# 2009: The Best
## *Men's Stage Monologues and Scenes*

Edited and with a Foreword
by Lawrence Harbison

MONOLOGUE AND SCENE STUDY SERIES

A SMITH AND KRAUS BOOK

Published by Smith and Kraus, Inc.
177 Lyme Road, Hanover, NH 03755
SmithandKraus.com

First Edition: October 2009
10 9 8 7 6 5 4 3 2 1

Cover design by Dan Mehling, dmehling@gmail.com
Text design by Julia Hill Gignoux, Freedom Hill Design and Book Production

The Scene Study Series 1067-3253
ISBN-13 978-1-57525-760-0 / ISBN-10 1-57525-760-2
Library of Congress Control Number: 2009936730

NOTE: These scenes are intended to be used for audition and class study; permission is not required to use the material for those purposes. However, if there is a paid performance of any of the scenes included in this book, please refer to Rights and Permissions pages 149–152 to locate the source that can grant permission for public performance.

# CONTENTS

iii

## SCENES

# Foreword

This year Smith and Kraus has decided to combine its annual best monologues and best scenes anthologies. The scenes included in this book are either for two men or for one man and one woman. The latter are scenes in which the male role is predominant.

Here you will find a rich and varied selection of monologues and scenes from plays that were produced and/or published in the 2008–2009 theatrical season. Most are for younger performers (teens through thirties), but there are also some excellent pieces for men in their forties and fifties, and even a few for older performers. Some are comic (laughs), some are dramatic (generally, no laughs). Some are rather short, some are rather long. All represent the best in contemporary playwriting.

Several of the monologues are by playwrights whose work may be familiar to you, such as Don Nigro, A. R. Gurney, Sam Bobrick, Terrence McNally, Adam Rapp, Steven Dietz, Itamar Moses, Stephen Belber, Keith Reddin, Naomi Iizuka, Michael Weller, Roberto Aguirre-Sacasa, Richard Vetere, Bruce Graham, Jacquelyn Reingold, Sam Shepard, and Nicky Silver; others are by exciting up-and-comers like Octavio Solis, Lydia Stryk, Michael Vukadinovich, Liz Flahive, John Kolvenbach, Sylvia Reed, Barton Bishop, Padraic Lillis, Michael Golamco, and Lucy Thurber. The scenes are by master playwrights, such as Itamar Moses, Noah Haidle, Aguirre-Sacasa, and Silver, and by exciting new writers, such as Saviana Stanescu, E. M. Lewis, Jonathan Rand, Kolvenbach, Golamco, Larry Kunofsky, and Susan Bernfield.

Most of the plays from which these monologues have been culled have been published and, hence, are readily available either from the publisher/licensor or from a theatrical bookstore such as Drama Book Shop in New York. A few plays may not be published for a while, in which case contact the author or his agent to request a copy of the entire text of the play containing the monologue that suits your fancy. Information on publishers/rights holders may be found in the rights and permissions section in the back of this anthology.

Break a leg in that audition! Knock 'em dead in class!

*Lawrence Harbison*
*Brooklyn, New York*

# MONOLOGUES

# ACCORDING TO GOLDMAN

## Bruce Graham

Dramatic
Gavin Miller, thirties to forties

> *Gavin, a has-been screenwriter, has left Hollywood and taken a job teaching screenwriting at a university. This is the first class of the semester, and he has just finished showing the students a 1940's black-and-white film.*

GAVIN: Yeah, I know. Black and white. Get over it.
(*He leans on his desk.*) Now, why did he show us scenes from this old movie, you're asking. Well, it's the first class and it eats up a lot of time, but more important — it's because movies were better built in the old days. Writers knew structure back then, first act, second act, third act — it's all there — better than any textbook. Until I write mine, of course. (*He looks out at them for a moment.*) OK, let's see hands — and be honest! How many of you think that your life would make a helluva movie? Come on . . . (*He zeroes in on one student.*) Be honest. (*The hand goes up, and he nods, satisfied.*) Much better. Just about everybody I've ever met thinks his or her life would make a great movie. How do I know? Very simple. Every time someone hears what I do for a living, they proceed to tell me that their lives would make a helluva movie. Oh, the wild and zany adventures you've had — the fascinating people you're related to . . . (*He smiles.*) Guess what? I hate to break it to you, but nobody gives a damn about your life's story, let alone wants to pay nine bucks on a Saturday night to sit through it. Unless, of course, your traumatic childhood memories included explosions, brief nudity, and a part for Brad Pitt. Fantasy! This is what the movies are all about. People in the movies are better looking than we are . . . drive nicer cars . . . have better sex and are braver than any of us will ever be. That's why we pay good money to spend time with them and not you or your relatives.

# ALOHA SAY THE PRETTY GIRLS

## Naomi Iizuka

Dramatic
Derek, late twenties

*Derek is trying to write the great American novel and failing miserably due to a massive case of writer's block. In an effort to spark his imagination and discover himself, he breaks up with his girlfriend, leaves home, and boards a plane for the tropics. Once he touches down on the other side of the world, things begin to get very strange. Nothing and no one is what it seems, and Derek is left trying to make sense of a world that's puzzling, magical, menacing, beautiful, and completely unpredictable. This monologue occurs as Derek is beginning to unravel in his new locale.*

DEREK: OK, aloha. I've been thinking about this. Aloha means good-bye, but it also means hello. It actually means a lot of things. it's all about how you say it. You could say it as you're going, and the plane's about to take off, and you're waving, and you could just say aloha, just let one fly, and if you were to say aloha like that, with the wave and everything else, I think everyone would be pretty clear about your meaning, but now let's say you're arriving here, you know, in Hawaii, and the airplane touches down, and the door opens, and suddenly you get a whiff of that air, do you know what I'm talking about? Warm and moist and all smelling of plumeria, which is like a kind of orchid, I guess, and you're making your way down the little metal staircase, and the light is so bright, it's blinding, and you're reeling from the smell of orchid, it's like the whole world is one big, bright orchid somebody just shoved in your face, and you are so overwhelmed, you don't even know what to do with yourself, and so what you do is you trip, you don't mean to, but you do, you just kinda fall, you fall down, and before you know it, you're flat on your back on the tarmac, and this pretty girl is standing over you, and maybe she's wearing a grass skirt, or maybe not, but it doesn't really matter 'cause the key detail, all right, is that around her neck, she's wearing all these leis, and before you know it, she's slipping one of her leis over your head, and you're overcome with this smell of orchid, and she's leaning real close, and whispering in your ear: aloha. She says, aloha. And I don't think it means good-bye in this situation. I think it means something else.

# AMERICAN TET
Lydia Stryk

Dramatic
Danny Krombacher, midtwenties

*Danny is a military policeman on duty at a prison in Iraq. While his family eagerly awaits his return home on leave, Danny struggles with things he has seen and done on the job. In this monologue, he addresses an imaginary tribunal, obviously aware that he may be called to account at a later date.*

DANNY: Explain it, sir? The first thing you have to understand is that this is someone who wants you dead, sir. This is a terrorist. A terrorist is not human, sir. They don't deserve to be called human, sir. Or to be treated as such. Your heart gets filled with hate. Hate is a kind of white heat, sir. It is burning hot and ice cold at the same time. Burning and frozen. That's what hate is like, if I had to describe it. One thing I learned early on, sir, was never to look them in the eye. Never. And best of all is not to look at their face. Faces can be deceiving, sir. So we blindfold them and put hoods on them. To cover those faces. Then you're in no danger, sir, of looking into their eyes. So then it's just a body, sir. It's flesh. Like a corpse, that's still alive. I had no problem, sir, in kicking a terrorist until he stops. He has to be made to stop. He has to be made to obey. To listen up. To do what I say. It's funny what a body can take. Take the penis, sir. Or the balls. Take a simple finger, sir. For that matter. Or toes. You strip a body of clothes. Clothes conceal weapons. You don't know what they are hiding. Bodies are weapons. You strip them down. You search inside. Deep inside them, sir. Because you don't know what they are hiding.

   *(Short pause, as if answering.)* That's our job, sir. To find what they are hiding. Make them talk. Sometimes the secrets have to be pulled out from the deepest places. This can be tricky. Because you never draw blood, if you can help it. Blood is messy and has to be cleaned. And it leaves traces. When a man is hanging from his feet, sir. Everything rushes down and out. Which is convenient. But the screams are too loud. So

you stuff a rag in the mouth. The hands are tied behind the back. It doesn't take them long to choke to death. So you have to watch out. It's a fine art, sir, not to let them die. Because that's what they want. A lot of the time. Just to die and get it over with. *(Answering.)* If it were me, sir? . . . Sir, if I thought like that, I couldn't do my job. I'm paid to do my job. I didn't start this war, sir.

# AND THE WINNER IS
## Mitch Albom

Comic
Tyler, forties

*Tyler has arrived in purgatory (which looks rather like a traditional Irish pub) the night before his star turn at the Oscar ceremony. Seamus the bartender has been trying to apprise him of his current situation, but all he wants to talk about is his Big Night tomorrow night.*

TYLER: Anyhow, the Chippen-Cops was a franchise, and you don't fart at a franchise. Although I never liked being the Sassy one. I mean, who would? . . . These young actors — they're like locusts! I gotta do botox and tanning booths. He rolls out of bed all bronzed and smooth, like a goddamm Pillsbury biscuit. Anyhow, that all changes if I win this Oscar. They judge you on your performance, you know.

. . . *(Animated.)* Wanna hear how it happened? Here's how it happened! I told Teddy, "Enough Chippen-Cops!" Make me blind!

. . . Blind. Deaf. Dumb. That's how you win an Oscar.

. . . And then, out of the blue, *The Wind and the Fury*, a small art flick, right? They got this guy in it — "serious" actor, nothing but Circle Rep and Royal Shakespeare and PBS Playhouse and all that non-paying shit — and he's playing this gimpy Civil War courier, one-legged, partially blind, speech impediment.

. . . I know! Jackpot! So this Circle Rep guy, two days before shooting . . . he drops out! *He drops out!* A gastric ulcer! Serves him right. All that Richard the Third . . . "This is the winter of our discontent, made glorious summer by this Duke of York." Yeah, yeah, yeah. So . . . he drops out, goes back to Woodstock with his Shakespeare and his Maalox, and Teddy gets me into *The Wind and the Fury* — at a reduced rate, I might add — and I play the one-legged Civil War courier with the bad eye and the speech impediment, and I play the SHIT out of that part, great reviews and NO box office — the critics love that, it's like they're adopting a puppy — and then, last month, the morning of the nominations, I get that call at five-thirty A.M.

. . . *(Not breaking stride.)* I pretended I was asleep. Everybody does. *(Mocking.)* "Oh, I completely forgot it was Oscar day." BULLSHIT! There isn't an actor on the planet who isn't staring at the phone by four A.M.! I, personally, had to take two Valiums just to get through the night.

# BACK BACK BACK
Itamar Moses

Seriocomic
Kent, thirties

> *Kent is a star baseball player. He is talking to a rookie named Adam*
> *who is very nervous about talking to reporters, advising him how best to*
> *handle them.*

KENT: OK. I played for Team U.S.A. in eighty-four. Right here, actually, all
the games were in this park, which, first of all, was a real head trip for a
bunch of amateurs, but it was also the first time I really had to do any
of that stuff, be on TV, deal with media, any of that, on any kind of big
scale, and this was, I don't know if you remember, but there was a boy-
cott, like, because we didn't go to Moscow the time before, all the Soviet
countries didn't come here, and President Reagan's there, and everyone's
asking all these questions. And I'm shy. I'm a really shy person when it
comes down to it. So that's also when I figured out this trick. Because,
basically? Anything these guys ask you, you can usually answer it in a
word, or like a few words, but you could also pad that simple answer out
to three, four, five times longer. And they think you're just being thor-
ough or complete or something good? But what you're really doing is
you're using your answer as a way of taking the time you need. To get
ready. For the next one. "Hey, Adam, how do you hope to play?" "Uhh.
I want to play well." No. "What I'd really like is I'd like to be able to contribute and to make a real contribution. Here on the ball club." They
know what you want to contribute to. You don't have to say ball club.
Say it anyway. "Because I want to be able to give something back to all
the great fans who have made me feel so welcome since I came here to
play and to all my great teammates because you know we've got a great
team here." They do know. They are professional sportswriters who
cover your team for a living. Say it anyway. "Because, hey, we've got such
a great bunch of guys here, Ricky and Dave and Big Dave," see, because
they also like it when you refer casually to the other people on the team
by their first names, like you're all really tight, for some reason they love
that, "and Raul, and of course Kent, it's great to have Kent to look up
to, to have a real star and a real hero in the clubhouse to model yourself

on." And, by the way, if you listen to Raul talk to them, this is the exact opposite of what he does, but, fact is, you're the one who gets to set the pace. Because they don't get to ask the next question whenever they want. They can only ask it when you stop talking. And you do not stop talking until you're ready. And it's not so you have time to dwell on what you said before, and it's not because you're planning, you can't, 'cause you don't know what's coming. It's taking the time. Just to stay in that one question till you are done with it. You hold that fucking moment till it's over. *(Pause.)* Do you understand what I'm saying to you?

# BACK BACK BACK
Itamar Moses

Dramatic
Raul, thirties

*Raul is a major league baseball player. He is talking to the press and has
a chip on his shoulder about what he considers their negative coverage
of him, as well as what he and many of the players view as illegal col-
lusion among the owners to limit what they pay to free agents.*

*(It's May 1995 in New England. A locker room. Raul is at his locker, wear-
ing a towel. He is talking to the press. During the following, he changes into
yet another different team's uniform, and by the end of the speech, he is fully
dressed.)*

RAUL: I mean, it's complicated. But what I wish? Is I really wish more of the
top guys had been able to see, you know, the link, between a salary cap
and revenue sharing, by which I mean the practice of sharing revenue,
which, combined with a cap on salaries, could have prevented this whole
thing. But instead, we cut off the whole season and everybody in the
whole country's feelings about the entire game of baseball are jeopar-
dized because of just the greed that everybody exhibited through the
whole thing. But you know what, guys? I think? A great player? Who is
playing great? Could really help the game to bounce back from all this.
But, see instead, with you guys, it's, you know, it's Bad Boy Raul is in
town, and what kind of trouble is he gonna get into on the club, and
what kind of shenanigans is he going to be involved in, and once again
that's the story, and, frankly, I mean, I just, I find it kinda interesting,
why a guy like me, or Barry, is the bad guy all the time, while another
guy might not be the focus, and why that might be, instead of, oh, let's
knock Raul again, because had some stupid injuries he could have
avoided, or got hit on the head by a fly ball one time, or was maybe
caught five years ago for speeding, or, whatever, crashing, because he was
worked up from a fight he had with his wife at the time that, OK, maybe
it got a little physical, but which was the whole reason he was speeding
in the first place, and we've been divorced four years now, so leave it
alone already, or who had a handgun one time in his car that the cops

only even found because he left it on the seat after he accidentally, OK, accidentally parked in the handicapped spot at a hospital, which was the only reason they even looked, like it's not like I was even holding it! Because if that's the kind of thing that you guys want to write about, again, this year, instead of something positive? Then you guys go ahead and write about that. And I'll just know? In my heart? That that tells me a hell of a lot more about you guys than it says anything at all about me. Now if you'll excuse me, I have a game to play.

# BAGGAGE
Sam Bobrick

Comic
Jonathan, forties

*Dr. Jonathan Alexander, a twice-divorced therapist, is addressing the
audience about the futility of the relationship of the play's main characters, Phyllis and Bradley, even if the play does end happily.*

JONATHAN: How do you do. I'm Doctor Jonathan Alexander, a professional,
licensed psychologist with degrees from several prestigious universities, a
BA, an MA, a Ph.D, etcetera, etcetera. I deal mainly in complex coun-
seling and have written a number of books on the subject, among them
*Couples in Conflict, Couples in Combat,* and the recently published *Couples in Hell.* All of them about nipping bad relationships in the bud.
What you are watching, obviously, is a story about two people who are
absolutely so wrong for each other, but nevertheless become involved
with each other and most likely at the end of the play end up together.
A wonderful, neat little story that we seem to encounter in movies and
plays over and over and over again. Frankly, for my taste, I find these sort
of stories a bit trite, but that's not important. What is important is that
they are really very misleading and does you, the audience, a great dis-
service. Ladies and gentlemen, in my professional and knowledgeable
opinion, you are watching a train wreck about to happen. I don't care
how the play ends, this is a relationship that won't and can't work and
unfortunately two years down the line I'm afraid they're going to find
that out. I know what I'm talking about. I've been down this road several times myself with the wrong partner. That's why I got into this line
of work in the first place. Phyllis and Bradley are two very, very troubled
people who, if they had any common sense, would get out of each others lives as fast as they can. Let's start with Bradley. Bradley! Just his name
makes me shudder. It really says it all, doesn't it? Angry, confused, and
whiny. God, I just hate to see a man cry. Certainly, there are times when
it can't be helped, like over the loss of a loved one or when your favorite
baseball team loses the World Series, but for the most part it shows a def-
inite lack of confidence and control, not really a desirable attribute in a

man. And as for Phyllis, I, myself, would rather get run over by a semi-truck than get involved with someone like her. I've seen controlling women before, but she takes the cake. Strong, domineering, opinionated, she would rather live anyone else's life but her own. What the hell can these two very troubled and contradictory people expect from this sort of union? What happens after they marry and are up to their necks in kids and house payments and car payments and school tuitions and insurance payments and realize they are both now living a life of unfulfillment, unhappiness, and ulcers? The point I'm making is that life is not a play. You've got to think past the happy ending, for crying out loud. If two people aren't right for each other at the beginning of the relationship, they haven't got a prayer in hell of working it out down the line. I'll have more to say about this as the evening progresses. Anyway, Phyllis and Bradley have eaten and they're on their way back to her place, so I'd better get going. Oh, by the way, at the end of the play, you'll have an opportunity to buy all three of my books in the lobby. Thank you.

# BILLBOARD
## Michael Vukadinovich

Comic
Damon, twenties

> *Damon is speaking to his best friend, Andy, who has recently had a corporate logo tattooed on his forehead for a great deal of money, much to Damon's dismay. It's now late, and they've had a great deal to drink. It's the end of an absurd argument about the tattoo.*

DAMON: You know that whole Christo and Jean-Claude thing they did in Central Park? I remember when they were showing it on the news, and I saw this homeless guy in the background just staring up at one of the flags. Man, he must have been wondering how they could spend so much money to decorate a park full of homeless people. Sure, covering Central Park in orange curtains may be great and beautiful and all that, but man, what if they had used those millions of dollars to buy every homeless person in New York brilliant orange suits? Then everyone would know who was homeless from blocks away and could take them out to eat. No one would be afraid to take them to a restaurant because the homeless would be the best-dressed people in the city. You know what we should do? We should go cash that check and buy suits. Fucking Armani. Then we'll go to the nicest, most expensive bar we can find in this city. And we'll go up to the hottest girl we can find, and we'll buy her a drink. The fanciest stuff they have. And we'll just sit there and talk to her. Classy. And then we'll thank her and say good night and drive to the nastiest, diviest bar we can find. And we'll go up to the dirtiest, ugliest woman we can find and buy her a shot of cheap whiskey. And we'll talk to her. Then we'll say good night to her. That's what we should do. In Armani suits.

# DR. JEKYLL AND MR. HYDE
## Jeffrey Hatcher

Dramatic
Jekyll, thirties to forties

*Dr. Jekyll is a charismatic scientist, here examining the brain of a re-*
*cently deceased woman. He is talking to Sir Danvers Carew, the head*
*of a hospital where the woman's body has been brought, who has ques-*
*tioned Jekyll's conclusions about the cause and circumstances of the*
*woman's death.*

JEKYLL: Sir Danvers, you say the woman's brain is small. Of course it's small,
she's been dead three days with no hydration, it's shrunk! As any of ours
would shrink in similar circumstances, as your brain would shrink, if
further shrinkage were possible. As for some parts of her brain being
dwarfed, as you put it, that's because the body was obviously improperly
stored, in a tilted position, causing what blood remained in the head to
gather on one side, thus bloating the tissue. As for what you call "her
sex," it's swollen because the woman was raped, and the "canine tears"
around her neck are not the result of teeth, but rather a clumsy attempt
to mask a murder by making it look like the attack of a dog. I'll wager
those are from boot nails or a cobble pick. As for the rest, including your
assumption as to the location of her soul, I leave to a higher knowledge.
Now cover her.

    . . . If you want lurid depictions, Sir Danvers, buy a postcard from
a Frenchman.

# DR. JEKYLL AND MR. HYDE
Jeffrey Hatcher

Dramatic
Jekyll, thirties to forties

*Dr. Jekyll is a charismatic scientist.*

JEKYLL: . . . "Sir Danvers." The fool! If he can't cut into it, he can't fathom it. He rails against voodoo and "savages," then stands before a hundred students and gives credence to all manner of superstitious — Utterson, I have seen in jungle clearings and island shores levels of understanding advanced beyond anything contemplated in a college lecture hall! I met a diviner in Suriname once who could calm his nerves by closing his eyes and humming a bird's song. A priest in a South Seas hut who, with one draw on a pipe of yellow smoke, left this reality for another plane, serene and at peace. There is a distinction between the brain and the mind!

. . . You find an open door. One no one knows about. And once you've crossed its threshold, you will find not one mind but *two*. Two streams within the consciousness, one on the surface, the other subterranean. Utterson, think on how your flesh warms when a woman enters the room. Think on your fear when a hansom cab comes barreling 'round a corner, and you dash for safety faster than you thought possible.

. . . Our minds are fueled by blood and bile and secretions triggered by all manner of stimuli. Coursing through our veins is the river of our old ways, before man created morality, in the time when humans hunted for food, killed for dominance, and copulated for pleasure. Morality harnessed our bestial instincts, but it did not kill them. If it had, there'd be no empire. They're all still deep inside us. We see hints, though, in the madman's eyes, the killer's glint, the rage of a drunken father who beats his child. If we could find the chemical balance that would isolate these rages, these horrors, wouldn't we pursue their cure?

# DUCK HUNTER SHOOTS ANGEL
## Mitch Albom

Seriocomic
Sandy, thirties to forties

> *Jaded tabloid journalist Sandy is talking to a disembodied voice, ex-*
> *plaining what he does for a living. He sees himself as a once-legitimate*
> *writer who has sacrificed his art for money.*

SANDY: Crap. I write crap.

. . . Explain crap? Well. If I had a dictionary — *(Produces dictionary,*
*holds it open.)* Ah. Let's see . . . Crap. One. Nonsense. Drivel. Two. A lie.
An exaggeration. Three. Rubbish. Junk. As in "Will you clean up that
crap?" *(Closing book.)* Well, no. You see. That was the problem. I
wouldn't clean it up. I just made more of it. When the old crap went dry,
I made up new crap. I was a crap recycler. I should have had a red plastic bin outside my office door: "Crap."

But you asked me what I do, I write crap . . . because I'm *supposed*
to write crap. For a supermarket tabloid, called the *Weekly World and*
*Globe.* It's not even a *good* tabloid. It's like ten notches BELOW the *Na-*
*tional Enquirer.* You know how hard *that* is to pull off?

. . . It's not that I didn't have higher aspirations. I mean, honestly
. . . Does anyone grow up wanting to write for the *Weekly World and*
*Globe?* It comes out *twice a week!* They were gonna call it the *Bi-Weekly*
*World and Globe,* but the owners thought that sounded gay. Or bi. Not
that our readers know the difference. We sell four hundred thousand
copies each week — twice a week — and I fill the pages. I write about
aliens taking over the White House and three-headed babies who speak
three languages. I give them half-boy, half-wolf creatures that hide inside
shopping carts at the Piggly Wiggly. I give them . . . "Man, eaten by alligator, comes back in alligator's body, takes revenge on swamp." You
wouldn't believe how well that story sold . . . You asked me what I do.
This is what I do: I write crap, for the *Weekly World and Globe,* which
comes out twice a week. I don't do it for art. I don't do it for satisfaction.
I do it for this . . . my paycheck. Which comes out once a week.

# EQUIVOCATION
Bill Cain

Seriocomic
Cecil, forties to fifties

> *Cecil, prime minister of England, commissions a play from William Shakespeare (here called Shagspeare, one of the several known spellings of the name of this mysterious fellow). Cecil is looking for a talented hack to spread government propaganda through the popular art form of theater, and he thinks he has found such a hack in Shag. He genuinely admires Shag, not for his genius or talent but for his lack of a moral viewpoint, which is a big plus in the field of government propaganda. Cecil is delighted and astonished to find someone so like himself — a skillful manipulator of the common people.*

CECIL: *(Don't fuck with me.)* I am well-informed about your playwrights . . . I don't want Fletcher. I don't want Beaumont. I don't want *Johnson* or *Kyd*. I don't want any *bullshit* about cooperative ventures. I don't want to be told what you do or do *not* do. What I *want* is for you to write this play. . . . This is to be the official version of the event so it must last. Your works will last . . . Oh, yes. Of all the writers now writing, your work will last.

. . . Oh, yes — I knew that after your play about the moor . . . You took a very bold position. You told the moors they are nobel victims of a cruel white world. Then you had the moor disembowel himself for the entertainment of the white audience — and everyone — even the moors — were pleased.

*(Then.)* You did the same thing with the Jews. You told them they have a right to their age and then you told the Christians they have a right to take the Jews' money, baptize them against their will, and somehow everyone went away satisfied . . . It is an astonishing achievement.

*(With a growing edge.)* With every new play, you raise the bar in the art of cynical audience manipulation.

*(Then.)* You tell bloated kings they are to be pitied because they bear greater burdens than their subjects, and then you tell their starving subjects they have the dignity of kings — though, as I gather from this new

play — you know kings have none. You do all of this with a straight face and — somehow — everyone believes you.

*(Then.)* You have discovered what every leader from Jesus to James has sought in vain. You, Master Shagspeare, have discovered how to be all things to all men.

*(Admiration and disgust.)* To do this, you have made yourself a pure vessel. You have shat out of yourself any trace of personal belief — any hint of personality — any hope of truth — so that all that is left of you is endless and universal flattery. Since that will never go out of style, I believe your plays will still be being done —

*(Lavish guess.)* Fifty years from now.

# ESSENTIAL SELF-DEFENSE
Adam Rapp

Seriocomic
Yul, twenties to thirties

> *Yul is working as a padded dummy at a self-defense studio and is something of a crank. Here he is sharing his views on everything bad he feels about our contemporary culture with Sadie, a woman in the class who likes him.*

YUL: Welcome to America, enjoy the view of our manifold strip malls and roadside horror outlets.

. . . It means that the operators of the machine want you to be afraid so you'll buy more stuff. That's why every media outlet is so oversaturated with violence. They want us all to be good Americans. The directives don't come from a man with a little mustache standing at a podium barking out orders. It's much more subtle than that. Our totalitarian maniac is the invisible radio wave, the pixel on your television screen, the airbrushed cheekbones in the magazine ad. Take any four hours of network television and what do you see? Violent content interspersed with cell-phone commercials. And ads for fast food and chocolate bars and beauty products. If I buy that Kit Kat bar maybe I'll feel better. If I eat that quarter pounder with cheese then maybe I'll forget that I'm about thirty years away from dealing with my own sedimentary rot. Consumption equals comfort. The more comfortable we are, the less we question. The less we question, the more the machine can continue spinning on its deified industrial sprocket. The anesthetized don't want to know where the needle comes from; they just want to feel good.

# FAULT LINES
Steven Belber

Dramatic
Joe, forties

> *Bill and Jim are two lifelong buddies who are meeting in the backroom*
> *of a bar to catch up, having not seen each other in a while. Joe is some-*
> *thing of an intruder who has insinuated himself into their party and*
> *doesn't get the message that he's not welcome. It has become clear that Joe*
> *is in fact not there randomly. He has an agenda. Here, he is telling Jim*
> *and Bill, whether they want to hear it or not, what he has perceived*
> *about both of them.*

JOE: *(Strong, simple.)* You should stay. *(Bill stands there, unsure what to do.)*
And I'll tell you why. It's because you guys are at a *point* in your life. No?
You're at a *point* where . . . how do they say it? . . . where the plates are
*shifting.* That's where you are, Bill. *Jim's* kind of wishing he had a life
partner to go home to; *you're* thinking about having a kid. And *I'm* wondering what I'm doing with my divorced, graying, alimony-paying ass.
Plates are shifting. Things are getting *shifted.* No? It's a good time for
everyone to check in.
   . . . See . . . this isn't about fidelity as much as it's about *relationship.*
Those many, vital *partnerships,* which keep us going, but which need to
be checked in on *while* the plates are still in flux. *(Pause.)* This guy, for
example: Is he *really* the best friend? For the *next* forty-something? Is *he*
the submarine-sandwich bun upon which you're gonna unequivocally
lay your turkey slice? *(Pause.)* And if he is: What does that friendship require? To keep it alive. As time goes on.
   *(Joe looks meditatively up at the stars, which are blocked by the ceiling,*
*then continues.)*
   The reason plates shift, if I understand correctly, is that stress builds
up in the rocks. Which is the same for us. Lotta stress out there: "Commitment"; "career choice"; "should we have kids?"; "bizarre prostate behavior" — and when the stress gets to a threshold point, *two* things can
happen: we either make an adjustment of some sort and thus *ease* the
stress. *Or* — we fundamentally crack. What was once *one* solid land
mass . . . becomes *two.*

. . . Which brings me back to you. If your wife's messing around on you, especially if it's with *him*, you gotta view that as part of the bigger, *fundamental shift* picture: A symptom of tectonic, midlife stress.

. . . Meaning the question now becomes: Can you — can all *three* of you — survive the fissure? What*ever* that fissure may be. Can you stare down the width of an ever-yawning chasm — and still hold tight? *(Beat.) Or* — just let go. Of each other. *(Pause.)* Big questions, amigo.

# ⌐LT LINES

⌐phen Belber

Dramatic
Bill, thirties

*Bill is telling off Jim, who he thought was his best friend. Jim has run a strange "experiment" to test their friendship. Jess is Bill's wife.*

BILL: *(Quiet.)* I'm sorry your mother died and that you feel all alone in the world, Jim. *(Beat.)* That being said. *(Beat.)* If *this* . . . if your little experiment just now — if this was an attempt to find out the who and what of what you think you are — well then I will *tell* you what you are: You are a fucking cock-lick. You *are* a dick-lick. A scumfuck, college-age-fucking-chick-fucker. *That's* what you are, Jim. That is what you are. *(Pause.)* You stand over *there*, in the land of frozen adolescent bullshit-environmental-progressive fucking amoral *clowns*, stuck there forever and *cock-fucking* ever; and *I'm* over here, where life gets lived . . . *appropriately*. This is me, over here, and that's you. In the land of *shit*. Welcome to the reality check. You *are* that. *(Pause.)* And if Jess is over there *with* you, if she can't see that there are things in life *more important* than loyalty to friendship, if she finds your type of pathetic, morally fucking lax behavior *OK?!* — then let her be there, let the chips fall where they may. *I'll see her at the motherfucking courthouse!* Because I *could've* chosen to be with you, over there in the land of utter apathy and fuck-fuck, but I *didn't*. I chose honesty, Jim. I chose *truth*. Which is maybe what you wanted the whole time, all part of your plan to fucking fuck your way through fuckville with my beautiful fucking wife. And if that's the case, then go fucking nuts. Have a fuck fest, on me, seriously — fuck *you*, fuck *her*, fuck *off*, then fucking *die!* OK?! *(Shaking with conviction.)* Good-bye!

# 50 WORDS
## Michael Weller

Dramatic
Adam, mid- to late thirties

> *Adam, an architect whose business is foundering, has just confessed to his*
> *wife, Jan, that he is having an affair and plans to leave her. Here, he*
> *tells her why she has given him no choice.*

ADAM: Tim offered to buy me out. It's a good price, considering. I'm going
to accept. There's a teaching position at U-Penn, *tenure track,* they in-
vited me to apply. The department has some of my models on display in
the lobby — I had no idea. My work is actually still held in esteem here
and there, imagine!

. . . When we first fucked — me and Melinda, this time round I
mean, not the early encounters . . . she asked me something. "Do you
like what I'm doing right now." I misunderstood, I thought I'd failed to
notice something and she needed my praise, my support. The way you,
dear, need constant recognition for every inconsequential little thing you
do during the day, and I give it, and you sneer and pretend you're in-
sulted by the compliment, even though you're secretly pleased . . . But
her question, it hit me after a moment . . . she was trying to please me.
To make me happy. I forgot that women did that. I thought she was up
to something at first, you know, playing me. No. She was just . . . it was
her habit . . . pleasing a man was what she tried to do without thinking.
This may sound pitiful, Jan, but the sad truth is being treated that way,
being thought of as someone who should be pleased . . . it's phenome-
nal. It feels . . . I felt like a man. She made me feel like a man. Manly.
Male. God, you're right, it's wonderful to talk to a stranger, someone
you'll never see again. Imagine discovering at my age that a woman can
make you feel masculine. It's comical, really, how powerful that is. How
happy it makes her to use her power. And how happy her using it makes
me feel. As opposed to your power to make me feel like piece of shit. So,
thinking it over, the choice between giving a woman the power to make
me feel like shit, or to make me feel like a man, I've decided to spend
what's left of my good years on earth as a man, I've decided to spend
what's left of my good years on earth as a male. With Lindy. I was almost

about to turn my back on her. I was about to go out there and tell her I couldn't run off the way we'd planned — If this night had gone a different way . . . if you'd dug into your heart and found in your power to spend an hour or two simply being not thoroughly unpleasant . . . But instead — she and I are going to marry. It's what she wants, and I want. She has friends in Pennsylvania. They'll find us a place. We'll move there, far away from both the lives we've been trying to escape for years, because. Because. Because I hate you. Because I fucking hate how you refuse to let yourself be loved the way I wanted to, the way I could if you'd only let me. Because you made me want to do that for you more than anything on earth, then refused to let me do it.

# FROM UP HERE
## Liz Flahive

Dramatic
Charlie, seventeen

*Charlie has run up to the bus stop after seeing Lauren, fifteen, the object of his affection. It's early morning, before school. They've never really talked before.*

CHARLIE: You're a sophomore, right? Kenny Barrett's sister? *(Beat.)* Charlie. *(Beat.)* Senior. *(Beat.)* You going to the dance on Friday? *(A pause.)* People say you fucked two guys at Kristi Shinnick's party last weekend? Did you know people are saying that? *(A pause.)* David Blitzstein said the minute he put it in you, you started crying. Did he hurt you? *(Beat.)* Because it's only supposed to hurt the first time. I mean, it's not like I know, but I do because I talk to girls and they tell me stuff like, well not exactly what happens. I don't press for details because it's private — it's not that, but I have close girl friends, not girlfriends but we talk about sex. Not just about sex, but it's well, it's topical. Mostly sex is just topical, it's not paramount, not yet, anyway, because it's all just started or not started or not that good, but I guess it's safe to assume it will become a serious variable. At some point. But sex is not the most important thing, and I think a lot of people feel compelled to decide what that most important thing is, especially right now. I don't understand it, ordering the importance of everything. Like how everyone's all obsessed with class rank, who's number twenty, who's right up next to you at nineteen. And fine, I think it's good to know where you stand and but it's like everyone is so hung up on trying to get the least important things to matter the most. Whatever. But, see, I love walking around, knowing what I want. That's actually useful. To think about something and really want it. And then you see it and knowing it actually exists is . . . It's this feeling like I'm looking at everything through one of those cardboard tubes, the ones that hold paper towels and everything's all . . . *(Makes a circle with both his hands and extends one out like a handheld telescope.)* And I know what I want is to stand next to you and talk to you. Here I am. Doing exactly what I want. So this. Yeah. This is such a great day. Already. And it's pretty early. *(Beat.)* Hey. *(Beat.)* Bus.

# GOOD BOYS AND TRUE

Roberto Aguirre-Sacasa

Dramatic
Shea, thirties to forties

*Shea is the athletic coach at an exclusive Catholic boys prep school. A tape has been found that shows a boy forcing a girl to have sex with him, and Shea believes that one of his students is that boy. During gym class, a boy has asked him why everyone is making such a fuss over this tape. Here, Shea responds.*

*(Shea enters, blowing his whistle. He is standing in front of his class, talking to them.)*

SHEA: Two lines, gentlemen! Now, before we divide into teams, there's something requiring our immediate attention. *(He dives in.)* Today, this morning, Father Lawton called me into his office and informed me that he had received several *distressing* phone calls from concerned parents. From the mothers and fathers of some of your fellow students, freshmen and sophomore boys. Who told them they had heard rumors about a videotape which showed one of their classmates . . . being *intimate* with a young woman. As well as about a screening of said videotape on school grounds. When Father Lawton asked me if I knew anything about these *distressing* accusations, I was *ashamed* to have to tell him that I *did*. That I had, in fact, found and confiscated the tape, and that I was in the process of investigating the situation, which I will continue to do. *(Beat.)* Father Lawton has asked me to talk to the junior and senior classes and to ask anyone with any information about who made this tape — or who took part in this supposed screening — to step forward. Gentlemen — Father Lawton is so *perturbed* by these allegations, he has decided that until the person or persons involved step forward, you are *all* on probation. In other words: No extracurriculars for any and all upperclassmen, and — *(The tiniest hitch in his voice.)* — no sports. No practicing, no scrimmaging, no playing — *NO GAMES!* Therefore, my *personal* advice to whomever participated in this affront? Step forward with whatever information you have — receive your punishment — and let the rest of us continue with our year and our season. Mr. Simmons

— would you mind telling me what St. Joseph's mission statement is? Which you were asked — *(Takes in the entire class.)* which you were *all* asked — to commit to memory freshman year? "To be good boys and true. To strive towards competence, courage, and compassion always. To become men of faith and to live as men for others." And the First Principle of Jesuit Spirituality? *Cura Personalis:* "The person in front of me is the most important person in the world." *(Beat.)* Fifty push-ups, gentlemen! What's so *awful*, Mr. Simmons, is that there is *nothing* courageous or compassionate about what was done to this young lady on that tape. It was a — a demeaning, shameful, and exploitative act involving some or many of you. And *that*, Mr. Simmons, you'll pardon my language, is the *big* fucking deal.

# HENRY AND ELLEN
## Don Nigro

Comic
Henry, forty-one

> *Henry Irving, the last of the great Victorian actor-managers, is giving
> notes to his cast on the stage of the Lyceum Theatre in London, after a
> rehearsal for their production of* Hamlet *in which Henry plays the lead
> and directs. Henry is stern and a perfectionist, but he softens his criti-
> cism with wry but genuine compassion and a dark sense of humor.
> He's a very good director.*

HENRY: So. What else? I do wish the gravedigger would try to avoid mugging. We must resist the temptation to play him like old Yorick. He's an amusing fellow, and quite subtle, in his own way, but he's not the court jester; he digs holes for a living, and this has made him somewhat philosophical, and that's what's funny, the juxtaposition of his rather gruesome vocation with his tendency to philosophize. The humor grows from that, it's not superimposed upon it, yes? And it would be most helpful if the Queen would attempt not to tread upon Hamlet's foot as she bounds gracefully off the bed. I need that foot for the sword fight, dear. Um. I don't think Rosencrantz needs the extra padding in his tights. It's most unseemly, son, and tends to draw the attention of the ladies away from Hamlet, and we can't have that now, can we? Laertes, extra sword practice. It is my dream to expire on the stage, but not just yet, I think. Props, the blood still looks like vomit, and it comes out all lumpy. Can't we do something about that, please? Claudius, do try not to make everything sound like some sort of general announcement. It mustn't seem as if he's constantly bellowing into somebody's ear trumpet. The audience isn't deaf, at least not when they come in, most of them, I hope. Polonius, do make an effort to stay awake while I'm talking, there's a good fellow. Set an example for the patrons. So. In general, you've done remarkably well, considering, and I believe in fact we may be in some danger of having a rather good show. Tomorrow is dress rehearsal. Come well rested. I think that's all. Thank you.

# HENRY AND ELLEN
## Don Nigro

Dramatic
Henry, fifty

> *Henry Irving and Ellen Terry are the two greatest actors of their time, and
> they have had great success at Henry's Lyceum Theatre. They have been
> lovers for some time and care very deeply about one another, but they are
> in the midst of a quarrel that greatly disturbs both. Ellen has grown up in
> a family of famous actors and largely took the theater for granted until
> working with Henry renewed her joy and sense of wonder there. She wears
> her heart on her sleeve, has tremendous natural instincts as an actor, and
> is now excited about doing new plays by Shaw and Ibsen, instead of the
> melodramatic old clunkers with which Henry has had so much success.
> Henry hates Shaw for ridiculing him in his reviews and is deeply jealous
> of Ellen's epistolary flirtation with him. But Shaw's point is that the great-
> est actor of his time should not be wasting his abilities doing creaky old
> conventional plays, and Ellen very much agrees. She is also mystified as to
> why Henry does cigar ads to make money and then keeps old actors on the
> payroll he doesn't really need. Henry is trying to explain to her, much
> against his will, why he has become who he is.*

HENRY: Do you know, when you left me there on the bridge tonight, I was
reminded of another opening night, my first really triumphant night,
the opening night of *The Bells*. I was very excited that night. Terrified,
then increasingly confident, and then exultant. Extremely emotional, if
you can imagine that. I was riding home in a carriage with my wife after
the performance. My wife had never approved of my profession, and to
be fair to her, I had not seemed to be doing particularly well in it up to
that point, but I had fought hard to get this play on, and I had rehearsed
it like a madman, with a total obsession, and had given that night what
seemed to everyone, even the critics who had been most hostile and
brutal to me previously, to be a brilliant performance, and I was triumphant. For the first time in my life, after many years of the most hu-
miliating struggle imaginable, I was finally proclaimed a great actor.
After all the years of poverty and rejection, my future at last seemed secure. I had never wanted anything so desperately in my life as I wanted

that night for my wife to acknowledge, in the midst of my great triumph, that all my struggle had been worth it, that I had after all some value as an artist and as a person. I sat there in the carriage beside her, on the way home, and she was silent for the longest time, I hoped because she was moved, and because she finally understood what all the years had been about, and was trying to find just the right words to tell me. So I sat waiting, in the dark, the silence broken only by the sound of the horses' hooves on the cobbles, my heart pounding, filled with so much love for her and for my difficult profession, wanting so badly for her to finally understand my joy in it, to be able at last to share it with her, and finally, my dear, beautiful wife turned to me, and she looked me in the eye and said, Does this mean you're going to keep on making a fool of yourself in front of all those people for the rest of your life?

*(Pause.)* I asked the driver to stop, got out of the carriage, closed the door, sent the coach on home with her, and I have never again to this day seen my wife or spoken one word to her. I walked back to the theater through Kensington Gardens, on a night very much like this one, quite alone. The night of my great triumph, you see. Our victories, as few as they are, hard earned as they may be, tend to find us, like our defeats, utterly alone, totally isolated. And walking back here to your house, in the cold and the dark and the wet, I thought of the pain you must be feeling, and I was reminded of that night, the last night of my life in which I allowed myself the kind of emotional relationship to life offstage that you have. I save all that now for my work. You do not. I am not so much cold, I think, as pragmatic. But perhaps you are right. It was cruel not to say something to you. But I was cruel in Hamlet's fashion, in order to be kind. And artistically it was justified by your performance, which neither I nor anybody else who saw it will ever forget. But personally I see now that it must have caused you a great deal of genuine anguish, and for that I am very sorry.

# A HOUSE WITH NO WALLS
## Thomas Gibbons

Dramatic
Salif, sixties

> *Salif Camara, an African-American political activist in his sixties, publicly denounces a museum's description of a building that once housed nine of George Washington's slaves as the "servants' house."*

SALIF: "Servants' house"! Those are the words Cadence Lane and this museum use to describe the house that stood on this site. Two simple words, but they contain an entire history — the history of this country's deception and denial. The people who lived in this house weren't ladies' maids and gentlemen's butlers. They weren't paid for their labor. They weren't free to come and go or look for other employment. They weren't recognized as human beings. This house held slaves. Enslaved Africans kept in chains by George Washington. Are we going to let Cadence Lane and this museum lie about the reality of their lives? You've seen Cadence Lane on TV. You've heard about her book. She says this house has no meaning any more. She says racism has been uprooted from this country's soil. She says our struggle is over — let's forget the past and enjoy the land of milk and honey. Brothers and sisters, we all know the truth. We know America still has a long way to go. We know that a people who forget their past will never be able to find their future. Until we reclaim the memory of our enslaved ancestors, we can never be truly free. So we demand that this house be rebuilt, just as it once stood. To honor the nine souls who lived here. To remember what they endured. And to stop Cadence Lane — or anyone else — from lying about them.

# HUMAN ERROR
## Keith Reddin

Dramatic
Erik, late thirties to early forties

*Erik is a crash-site investigator for the National Transportation Safety Board. He has spent his life skimming by, never really committing himself. Here he talks to Miranda, who is in the shower, about his failed marriage and his inability to connect with his daughter. We're not really sure, though, whether Erik is speaking to Miranda or to himself.*

ERIK: You know what? I was supposed to call my daughter this morning. I have a daughter, and it's her birthday, and I promised I was going to call her this morning. Before she went off to school. But obviously I haven't done that. I didn't call her because . . . well because I've spent the morning with you, Miranda. I suppose I'm not a very good father. I mean I'm not a bad father, I'm not what you'd call a negative influence, I'm not much of anything I suppose. I haven't seen her in over a year. We parted ways, her mother and I, parted ways several years ago. I mean we decided it would be better not to be together, perhaps we never should have been together in the first place, we probably shouldn't have had a child, but things happen, she got preggers, and at the time we both thought that would be the answer to everything, to all our problems, someone other than ourselves to focus on, because the truth of the matter was our marriage was floundering, but at the time we both thought having this child, well that would bring us together, recapture whatever "magic" had been lost over the years. But it didn't. And I wasn't a very good father, as I've said. Pretty soon I left. Packed my bags and moved to another city. Last time I saw her was . . . it was nearly the summer. I met her and her mother, my ex-wife, we met at this restaurant, this seafood restaurant, and I tried to be . . . to be civil is the word, I suppose, but it was a dismal failure, it was terribly awkward, none of us knew what to say. Emma had trouble remembering me, I think, who I was exactly. Every few minutes I had to remind her I was her father, and I don't know about you, but I really hate fried clams, that was the special of the day, fried clams, and pushing these tasteless masses of breaded snot into my mouth I . . . I felt nothing for these people sitting across from me. Nothing but this sense of needing to escape. My child, the fruit of my seed, she was a total stranger, and suddenly I needed to get into my car, my rented car courtesy of the NTSB, and drive as fast and as far away as possible. So I made some lame excuse about having to make an appointment, wiped my hands with the Handi Wipe thoughtfully provided, kissed my daughter good-bye, and haven't seen them since. And I know I should feel something, some sadness, some terrible sadness at the state of my life, but I don't. I don't feel sadness at all, Miranda. No, I only feel this sense of relief. And a gnawing sense of guilt, that in some way I have gotten away with something, some terrible crime. And the thought occurs that perhaps I will never be caught and punished for my crimes. And I suppose if I believe in karma, the idea of karma, I suppose I will have to pay for these crimes in the next life. I suppose I will have to pay a heavy debt. But then I don't really believe in karma, so there we are.

# IRENA'S VOW
## Dan Gordon

Dramatic
Rokita, thirties to forties

> *Rokita, the highest-ranking gestapo officer in this area, is talking to*
> *Major Rugemer. Rugemer is a sixty-five-year-old German officer who*
> *runs a munitions factory, the hotel-like accommodations for officers,*
> *and the laundry that does the officer's clothes. Rokita is explaining to*
> *him that he should get new workers since within a few weeks they will*
> *have killed all the Jews in this area. He then rhapsodizes on the good*
> *German engineering of it all, the way you can take millions of people*
> *and get them used to standing in the lines that will lead to their deaths.*

ROKITA: Rugemer, it's because *you are* my friend that I'm telling you all of this
ahead of time. Don't rely on your Jews.
. . . Find substitute workers . . . Poles, like your servant girl over
there, northern types like us.
. . . Within a few months there won't be a live Jew left in this area.
Get used to the thought, Rugemer, and find replacements.
*(Rokita is a little tipsy and enjoying expounding on the genius of the*
*German plan to Rugemer.)* You have to stand in awe of it, you know,
Rugemer? It's not just the end result . . . the fact that finally we'll be free
of these vermin . . . but it's the how . . . it's the technique. It's the genius
of it. It's the application of modern science to a political and social
disease.
. . . But that's just my point. This isn't philosophy, it's . . . it's good
German engineering. Because there are *millions* of them, aren't there . .
. So how do you do it? By getting them used to following orders. At first,
nothing important . . . you have to wear a yellow star. Who's going to
fight about that, hmmm? Then you ban them from public parks. All
right, inconvenient, but no one's going to start a rebellion because they
can't walk their dog in the park. Then you ban the *dog*. Turn in your
dogs, you tell them. You have to have yellow passes. Next week, you ban
yellow passes, you have to have blue ones. Two days later blue ones aren't
important anymore, exchange them for red ones and they do! And each
time they do, they get that much more used to standing in lines and

doing exactly as they're told. Use them for laborers, by all means. Get some good out of them. They've been bleeding the German folk for years, so let them work. Make a pfennig or two off them. But you see . . . it's not just profit, it weakens them, too. Makes them less resistant. More pliable . . . more cooperative. Until we use them up. Until there's nothing left. Until what's left is just something . . . you'd throw into the incinerator.

. . . It's genius.

. . . My dear Rugemer, stop looking so glum. You think you have quotas? I assure you it is nothing compared to the pressure that we in the S.S. are under from Berlin. I have until July twenty-second to make sure that this entire sector is Jew-free. After that, if there's a single living Jew left in Tarnopol, I can kiss promotion good-bye. So, take my advice, major, get yourself some new workers.

# KICKING A DEAD HORSE
## Sam Shepard

Dramatic
Hobart Struther, forties

> *Hobart has trekked into the desert, but his horse has dropped dead on
> him. The entire play is a monologue addressed to no one in particular.
> The audience, maybe. Maybe the desert. Maybe to himself. Here, he
> launches into a tirade about how impossible it has become for him or
> anyone to "tame the West."*

HOBART: I do not understand why I'm having so much trouble taming the
wild. I've done this already. Haven't I already been through all this? We
closed the frontier in 1890-something, didn't we? Didn't we already ac-
complish that? The Iron Horse — coast to coast. Blasted all the buffalo
out of here. An ocean of bones from sea to shining sea. Chased the hea-
then Redman down to Florida. Trails of tears. Paid the Niggers off in
mules and rich black dirt. Whupped the Chinese and strung them up
with their own damn ponytails. Decapitated the Mexicans. Erected steel
walls. Sucked these hills barren of gold. Ripped the top soil as far as the
eye can see. Dammed up all the rivers and flooded the valleys for recre-
ational purposes. Run off the small farmers. Destroyed education.
Turned our children into criminals. Demolished art.

Invaded sovereign nations. What else can we possibly do?

# KING OF SHADOWS
Roberto Aguirre-Sacasa.

Dramatic
Nihar, teens

> *Nihar is a runaway. He is talking to a social worker who is trying to save him and her boyfriend, a cop. He has begged her to let him stay the night. He claims that he has escaped from a netherworld called the Kingdom of Shadows and that the King of Shadows and his consort, the Green Lady, are trying to find him and bring him back. Nihar is either a severely disturbed kid with a strange imagination or he is telling the truth.*

NIHAR: *(To Jessica.)* You've interviewed a lot of people like me? A lot of kids?

. . . And none of them ever talked about — the King of Shadows? Or mentioned him?

. . . Yeah, it's because nobody wants to hear that they're crazy, that they're making stuff up — (Though, in your defense, in the defense of people who don't know, the King of Shadows does kind of . . . defy belief.)

*(At least at the start of this story, Nihar speaks with confidence.)* The King of Shadows is a . . . a spirit, I guess, or a . . . creature, or monster, no one knows exactly. A demon, maybe. But he lives underneath us, underneath this world, in a place that's like . . . It's not heaven, it's not hell, but . . . another place that's all deserts and mountains and lakes and rivers and forests and grass and trees and rocks. Like a, a jungle. With palaces built of crystals, white and pink crystals.

. . . This is *Truth*. This is what's happening to us, every night.

. . . It's always night in this place, there's no sun, only a full moon, but it illuminates everything, like a blue sun, and it casts all these — That's why it's called the Kingdom of Shadows, because of what the moon does . . . *(Back on track.)* It's where he lives with his wife, who's called the Green Lady, because her skin, her hair, her clothes, everything, it's all green. And there are other spirits, other creatures, who are, like, their children. And they all have special powers — abilities — but the King of Shadows and the Green Lady are the most powerful. Like, they can become any animal they want, or water, or the air, they can fly, turn invisible, affect the weather — Like that rain, that storm — That was them throwing everything out of whack, disturbing everything — because they're trying to break through. *(Beat, explaining.)* It's kind of like they're punching at the wall that separates the Kingdom of Shadows from *this* world, and every time they hit it, there's a reverberation, an echo, and something happens with the weather. There's a lightning storm, or a tidal wave, or a forest fire, or an earthquake, or . . . something. And sometimes it's a big something, and sometimes it's . . . a breeze or a cloud or butterflies.

*(Beat.)* Originally, back in India, the Green Lady saw me through a . . . like this *portal?* Saw me with my real mom — (she was giving me a bath in a river) — and the Green Lady reached through — her arms are like tree branches — and pulled me into her world. I think to replace one of *her* children, the Green Lady's children, who had just died or something.

. . . It's true, I swear to God, it's true — *(Beat.)* After, like, years of living with them against my will, I got away, barely — (I could feel them chasing me, their breath on my neck, these fire-breathing wolves they keep as pets) — but I escaped from that realm to this realm.

. . . *(Beat, then he continues.)* When I first crossed over, I tried to tell other people the truth — some police, some caseworkers, I even called two reporters — but I got mocked — and beaten — on (seriously, that happened) — so I thought: "Forget it. Better just *lie.*"

. . . Their powers only work at night. Like, they can only cross over when it's dark, when the moon's shining . . . I know their secrets. I'm the only person who knows the truth.

. . . They're taking kids and holding them hostage. Because they're trying to replace me — or flush me out — or *something* — They're in the Realm of Shadows, probably in the work camps or the mines — I have all their names, I wrote them all down.

*(He pulls a notebook from his bag, offers it to Jessica.)* . . . The King of Shadows and the Green Lady keep coming, night after night, but once I get away, they'll stop. *(Beat.)* And, like I said, probably free the other kids.

. . . Look-please, Ms. Denomy — I don't think the kids are being hurt, I think they're probably . . . And I bet they'll be freed once . . . once . . . Once I get away for good, which is my ultimate plan, which I'll be able to do in . . . two nights — tomorrow night. Escape this world and cross over to another realm, where it's always day. Where there's no moon — no shadows.

# LAST OF THE BOYS
Steven Dietz

Dramatic
Jeeter, fifties

> *Jeeter and Ben are buddies who served together in Vietnam. Ben lives in a trailer, and Jeeter has come to visit him. Here, Jeeter is telling Ben that's he's worried about his relationship with his tattooed girlfriend, Salyer.*

JEETER: OK. Well. See — that's the thing: I haven't seen 'em. *Nobody's* seen them. She keeps 'em hidden all the time.

. . . Even in bed — making love to her — she keeps 'em covered — the lights out, the room dark — but one night, Ben, I wake up and I can't stand it anymore. She's dead asleep next to me — gloves, long sleeves, the whole deal — and I'm just — there's just this — I gotta just DO THIS — I gotta just do this THING, you know? So, I sit up. I get my flashlight out of my pack. And real slowly and real gently — because, I mean, I am *scared*, Ben, I am shaking like a drunk at Betty Ford — and so real easylike I pull back the sleeve of her shirt, just an inch or so . . . and I shine my light . . . and there on her arm I see a tattoo. *(Beat.)* And it is a *name*. It is a *man's name*. And it is not MY NAME — oh, no. And I am pulling back that sleeve another inch — and there is *another name. Another man's name*, Ben. Another man who is NOT ME. And then I get it: *These are the guys she's left behind. (Beat.)* And right away I pull her sleeve down and put my flashlight away, 'cause I don't want to *know* — I don't want to know how many *guys like me* she's left in her wake. I just know that, come what may: *I do not want to end up on that arm.*

# LAST OF THE BOYS
Steven Dietz

Dramatic
Jeeter, fifties

> *Jeeter and Ben are buddies who served together in Vietnam. Ben lives in a trailer, and Jeeter has come to visit him. Jeeter is telling his girlfriend, Salyer, about something that occurred in Vietnam that Ben would rather keep buried.*

JEETER: Ben's done a lot of amazing things. Has he told you about the three soldiers on a road? This was outside Oak To. *(To Ben.)* More of a path, really. Right? *(No response.)* Ben doesn't mind if I tell this. I'm his best friend in the world, *right? (No response.)* Little red dirt path through the jungle. Three grunts on patrol. They come across a body. Vietcong soldier. Seventeen, tops. Crispy-crittered by some napalm. But still alive. Some of his face gone. The soldiers spit on the ground. They all three know they gotta put this kid out of his misery. It's just a matter of who's gonna do it. The first soldier steps forward. "Fuck it" — he says — "I'll do it." Lifts his rifle to the kid's head — and then there's screaming. Someone running out of the jungle. An old woman. Hands in the air. Trying to stop them from doing this to — who? — her son, maybe? The soldiers are trying to shove her away but this *mama san* is wailing like a siren — and then she's *on top of her son.* Arms wrapped around him tight. And now the soldiers get it: She doesn't want him saved. She wants to *die with him.* Now, the second soldier steps forward — tries to pull the woman off her son, but she's hangin' on for dear life — back and forth they roll — this sobbing mass rolling up and down the road — the second soldier is screaming at the old woman: *"DIDI MAU, DIDI MAU"* — trying to wrench them apart — and crying — now he's crying — the second soldier is shaking and crying *and he still can't pry this mother from her son.* The third soldier steps forward, cigarette in his mouth. He lifts his rifle. Aims it at the woman's leg. Fires. Her leg shatters. Aims at the other leg. Fires. She right away goes into shock — eyes rolling back in her head — still clutching her son. The third soldier turns to the others. "She wants to die with him. Let her die with him." And he walks on. *(Long silence. Jeeter stares ahead, still "looking" at the story after he's told it.)*

. . . And when you ask him which soldier he was — he'll never tell. And I'll never tell — 'cause I would never do that to a friend.

. . . Told his dad, though. Wrote him a letter. Thought his dad would *understand.* His dad — the McNamara man, the win-at-any-cost man. But, when he got that letter, do you know what his father did? *(Salyer looks to Ben for the answer.)* Don't look at Ben. He doesn't know. His dad never told him this. *(Looks at Ben.)* Am I *right? (Ben just stares at him: Go ahead, you fuck, finish it.)* His dad took a red marker. And he wrote four words at the top of that letter: WHAT. IS. THE. PLAN? And he put that letter in an envelope —and he addressed it to the secretary of defense, his former boss, the honorable Robert S. McNamara. And that's how I found it. Lying in a pile of papers — in a basement — in Michigan. It was never sent. And right next to that letter, I found *a signed copy of McNamara's book* — with the same four words written at the top: WHAT. IS. THE. PLAN?

# A LIGHT LUNCH

A. R. Gurney

Comic
Marshall, twenties

*Marshall is a grad student in theater. His girlfriend, Viola, is a waitress at a theater-district restaurant in New York City where Beth, a lawyer, and Gary, A. R. Gurney's agent, are having a power lunch. Beth is representing a mysterious Texas businessman who wants to option A. R. Gurney's latest play, which is about President George W. Bush and our misadventure in Iraq. Viola has taken quite an interest in the play, hoping she can get herself cast in it, and has called Marshall to come over and offer his suggestions regarding the play. Here, he tells Beth and Gary what Gurney needs to do to make his play a true tragedy.*

MARSHALL: Never say anything is interesting in the theater, Beth. Never. It's the kiss of death. Why? Because "interesting" describes only an intellectual experience. Plays should always invoke an emotional response. They should be exciting, fascinating, or compelling. Let me say something else on this point. In our democracy, our leaders are quick to be celebrated for the good they have done, or what they *think* is the good they have done. They are eager to have buildings and airports and bridges named after them, sometimes even when they are still alive. The point is we go along with all that because they are responsible for bringing some good into the world. But what about the politicians who mess things up? Aren't they responsible, too? How do we deal with them?

Well, from what Viola has already told me, I'd say that's what Gurney is trying to do in his play.

Gurney's Bush would seem to be struggling to accept his own complicity in the damage he has done at home and abroad. Now that very struggle is something to be celebrated. It's what makes Greek tragedy so special, and Greek democracy so vital. The Greek tragic heroes, such as Oedipus or Ajax or Electra, may have done harm to their communities but in the end they acknowledge the damage they have done. They assume responsibility, take it onto their own shoulders, and because there is no ultimate or superior system of justice to punish them, they go on to punish themselves for their errors. And by punishing themselves, these tragic heroes — or heroines — purge the world of the corruption they have caused. And only then can the human community begin to recover its pride and confidence. Now, Gary, does George Bush do this in Gurney's play?

# A LIGHT LUNCH
A. R. Gurney

Comic
Marshall, twenties

*Marshall is a grad student in theater. His girlfriend, Viola, is a waitress at a theater-district restaurant in New York City where Beth, a lawyer, and Gary, A. R. Gurney's agent, are having a power lunch. Beth is representing a mysterious Texas businessman who wants to option A. R. Gurney's latest play, which is about President George W. Bush and our misadventure in Iraq. Viola has taken quite an interest in the play, hoping she can get herself cast in it, and has called Marshall to come over and offer his suggestions regarding the play. Here, he tells Beth and Gary how Gurney can fix the play's ending to make it more powerful.*

MARSHALL: You mentioned a movie, Gary. A film by the French director François Truffaut. I propose that Gurney consider a more appropriate film, and a more American one. David Lean's filmic masterpiece *The Bridge on the River Kwai*. It contains one of the great recognition scenes in twentieth-century drama. Toward the end of the film, Guinness suddenly confronts William Holden who has come to blow up the bridge that Guinness has so lovingly built as a proud example of Western expertise and knowledge.

(*He begins to act this out.*) "You!" Guinness says to Holden. Then he looks at his beautiful bridge just as a train full of Japanese soldiers is about to cross it and extend their occupation of Southeast Asia. And he suddenly recognizes that by building this magnificent bridge, he has only given aid and comfort to the enemy. So Guinness gasps and says, in horror, "What have I done?" Then Guinness is hit by a hail of bullets, and staggering sideways, he falls onto the plunger of the dynamite device to blow up the bridge. Now the question is, did Alec Guinness totally recognize his error and try to rectify it? Did he purposefully and heroically destroy his own handiwork? We'll never know. But we do know this: He becomes a far bigger man at the end. He becomes a man we admire because he says, "what have I done?" and he falls on the plunger. So we forgive his past delusions, with the result that the war soon ends, and the world is at peace, and Guinness gets an Academy Award.

See? Partial recognition and ambiguous death. That's what we want from Bush. Do you agree, Gary? Now remember I'm winging it here, but suppose Gurney has former President Bush fly to Iraq on what is described in the press as a personal, postelection, fact-finding tour. "I want to see firsthand what we accomplished on my watch," he reads from his teleprompter. So he flies to Baghdad first-class on Saudi Airlines and stays in the Green Zone. He inspects the mammoth fortress of our embassy still under construction and drives by our frightening, monolithic prison for terrorists and stops briefly at our military hospital where he chats with those few soldiers whose wounds don't require immediate evacuation. And he is so pleased with what he sees, these lucky soldiers and these imposing buildings, that he asks to be taken out of the Green Zone for a view of Baghdad and beyond. And so, sitting in his armor-plated Humvee, driving through the prearranged clusters of Iraqis stationed on either side, and peering through his thick security guard, he is shocked by what he sees. What shocks Bush is what he sees in people's eyes. The eyes of the Iraqi people. He expected cheers and the light of freedom shining in their faces. But he sees nothing but grim resentment and sullen anger and sad disillusionment. He also notices these qualities even in the faces of our own men guarding him. And he is also reminded of the expressions he has seen on faces back home, watching his motorcade down Pennsylvania Avenue when he left the presidency. And he glances back over his shoulder at the barbed wire of Green Zone, and our great, hulking edifices constructed to remain there forever — and he says quietly to himself, what does he say? Voilà? Exactly! "What have I done?" So there's your partial recognition, Gary. But by now his entourage is moving on, and up ahead he sees another cluster of Iraqis. "Are those Shiites or Sunnis or Al Qaidas?" asks our ex-president. The general says it's hard to tell. Ah, but within this group he sees one individual who is actually smiling and waving a small, torn American flag. "There! You see?" Bush says. "I want to shake that man's hand! I want to shake the hand of freedom." "I wouldn't, sir," the general says. "It's still dangerous out there." "Freedom is always dangerous," says Bush, and he steps out of his vehicle, brushes aside his security guard, and walks slowly toward the cluster of Iraqi citizens, and the tiny, torn flag fluttering feebly in their midst. Then suddenly shots ring out, and from all sides there is a hail of bullets — from the street, from the rooftops, from Bush's military security escort, and in the confusion — he's killed. By resentful Shiites. Or by angry Sunnis. Or possibly even by friendly fire. You see? An ambiguous death. And to bring down the curtain, you might suggest to Gurney that he have the Mormon Tabernacle Choir singing the Frank Sinatra song, "I Did It My Way."

# LOVE SONG
## John Kolvenbach

Comic
Beane, thirties

> *Beane is an introverted, morbid, and slightly lost character. He is speaking to his sister Joan, a hard-driving businesswoman, and her husband, Harry, ranting about what he believes is a conspiracy to make us buy things.*

BEANE: Have I Eaten in this *Life*time? Is there *proof* that I have *Ever* Eaten *Anything?* I am RAVISHING. I could eat a fucking *horse* — fucking eat a *horse* — eat fucking a *horse* — *any* of those. I was thinking on the way over, I'm lucky I didn't walk by any *meat*. I'm likely to drop down and eat a live *dog*. I'm half ready to grab a pigeon out of the *air* and eat its Breast. *(Beat.)*

    . . . *(Holding a carton of Chinese noodles.)* Can I eat this? Is there a fork? *(Then spying a bottle on the counter.)* Wine! "I am a Fool for wine, my friends, a Foolish Nit!" Can I drink this? I was talking to somebody the other day about the Redundancy of Glassware. *(Offering the bottle.)* (Sorry, does anybody want any? No?) About the *Conspiracy*, really, of the redundancy of just about *everything*, you know. You *buy* a glass thing to pour something *from* a glass thing *in*to when, there you are *with* a glass thing, cheers. *(Beane drinks from the wine bottle.)* Raincoats. You *buy* a water-resistant thing when you are in fact *already* a water-resistant thing, like we're gonna make a *purchase* that's gonna improve on *skin*, my *Ass*. I will walk naked down the street, and I will show you something about Water Repellence! *(He then eats noodles from the carton with his hands.)* It's a Conspiracy, The Goddamn Oligarchy that *insists we Buy* things. Look at this: Eat a noodle *from* a carton, when you already *are* a noodle eating a noodle from a carton! It is foolish food, my friends, when a noodle eats a noodle! *(Beat.)*

# LYDIA
## Octavio Solis

Dramatic
Claudio, early forties

*Claudio's daughter, Cecilia, was horribly injured in a car accident while out on a date with a boy and is now brain damaged. Here, Claudio tells the family maid, Lydia, what happened on that fateful night.*

CLAUDIO: I had a life *aya! Pero* the way you want and the way thing go: different. Rosa want her babies *que sean Americanos.* So here I am, not one, not the other, but a *como se dice,* a stone. A stone for them to make their own great *pinche* dreams. You want to know *que paso,* for reals? Three days till *la quinceañera.* Three days. Dinner set, salon reserve, the *comadres* all prepare. But *en medio de la noche,* everyones sleeping and me at work, Ceci y Rene out the window, and nobody hears *nada.* Why? Why push it the car in neutral down the street and then start it up? Why? *Con las alas del diablo* they tear down to the border en el West Side! Why! Three nights till the *quinceañera y se van,* they go somewhere too fast, *los pendejos* — too fast down *ese* dirt road by the border fence, and the tires are bald *en ese* Pontiac, you can't drive too fast in that car! Then something happen —

Rene's good, he drive good. But something make him miss the big curve, you have to slow down to turn, but Rene, he don't slow, he don't turn and — ! The car hit a pole *y ya. Mi* Cecilia, who is born on a full moon and dance the twist for me at six, who always understand me no matter what demon possess me, Cecilia Rosario Flores, her name on the cake of her fifteen year, fly through the windshield of the car into the cold hard ground fifty feet *en frente. Nada.* I ask him why. I ask him where the *chingados* they go. A million whys I ask him. He sit in the dirt and cry. He never answer, never.

# LYDIA
## Octavio Solis

Dramatic
Misha, twenties

> *Misha has a stormy relationship with his immigrant father, who is very stern with his family. Here he tells him that he is determined not to become like him.*

MISHA: Dad? . . . *Jefe? (No response.)* For what it's worth, it wasn't just Mom who raised me. It was you, too, asshole. You're half to blame. You're the idiot who knocked her up, right? Your last name is mine, too, right? Everything about me you resent is half of you too, motherfucker. The blood that came out my nose is yours, your spit in my face has my DNA all over it, and the shit I seem to give you time after time after *pinchi* time is the same shit you been giving me since the day I was born. So take some credit, Dad. I'm your son. I'm your decent, well-raised second son. You bred me with fists and belts and shoes and whatever else you could throw at me. You raised me to jump at the sound of your voice and the stamp of your foot. You taught me to cower and shake and cover my ears in bed at night so I wouldn't hear Mom screaming while you slapped her. You taught me shame. I should grow up to be a spiteful little fucker just like you, hating the world for the crap I bring on myself, piling some real hurt on the people who care for me most. Except you know what, I won't. No sir, I won't be you. I don't know what the hell I'm gonna be, and God knows I may turn out worse than I think, but I won't be you. Someday, not today, against my better sense, I'm gonna forgive you. You'll see.

# MARGO VEIL
## Len Jenkin

Dramatic
Roxanne's Boyfriend, thirties.

*He's calling Roxanne on the phone from Lithuania, where he's gone on a business trip. Everything has gone wrong, to say the least, and he's desperate to be sent money and certain papers.*

ROXANNE'S BOYFRIEND: *(On phone.)* Roxanne, Jesus. What took you so damn long to answer the phone? I need to talk to you. You won't believe the shit I'm in here. I met Mr. Secundas, turns out he's a fat guy in a bad suit and big moustache, picks me up at the airport in Vilnius, drives me to Kaunas telling dirty jokes in his lousy English all the way, and he checks me into this Hotel Palanga. I went out drinking that night — me, him, his partners, and three women look like cheap Russian whores. They order some kind of local liquor, and it hits me hard. Next thing I remember is I wake up at dawn on the banks of this stinking river they got here, in Nemanus, and two fishermen in a rowboat are pointing at me and laughing. Somebody stole my pants. The grass is wet, I'm soaked and shivering, my head is pounding, and then I realize my wallet was in those pants. And my room key. I got back to my hotel wrapped in a blanket I stole off somebody's washline. The room was stripped clean. My papers, passport, money . . . I got nothing. Nothing. It's fucked. The deal is fucked. It's my job. I'm gonna be fired.

. . . Look, Roxanne, you gotta fax me the papers on my desk, in the blue folder —

. . . Hotel Palanga, room 802, Kaunas. And money. I need money. Send me ten thousand dollars, in small bills. Western Union or something. Roxanne, you gotta do this or I am completely screwed. My balls are in the Lithuanian fire here. You know, this whole place is nuts. Before we go out last night, Secundas takes me into a church to show me some statue, and these old ladies are in there praying, and the priest comes out with a dead calf draped over his shoulders, drops it on the altar. He's saying something in this fucking language they got, and he tears the calf with his bare hands, ripping it apart. He ends up gnawing on a leg, blood all over his priestly vestments, and the old ladies just keep praying.

I swear these people worship the fucking seven dwarfs. Or the goddamn trees. Hey, Roxanne, I got you a present. At this street market. I'm not gonna tell you what it is. I know you're gonna like it . . . Look, you fax me those papers in the blue folder, and if everything goes OK, I'll be home by next Thursday evening. We'll go out somewhere. A movie or something. Roxanne, I love you. I gotta go.

# MARILYN GETS ICE CREAM
## Don Nigro

Seriocomic
Knees, thirties

> *Knees, a short, pudgy man in his thirties, sits on a bench in a Tastee-Freez ice cream shop in Phoenix, Arizona on an evening in March 1956, talking with his friend Jake, a young man in his twenties, who is sweeping up and getting ready to close for the night. Knees is the janitor at a local grade school, and has been telling Jake that a pretty second grade teacher has been fired, reported by someone for being "a bad influence on the kids," but has not yet explained what that means. Knees has also been telling Jake that not long ago Marilyn Monroe, who is in town filming rodeo scenes for the movie* Bus Stop, *has made an appearance at this very Tastee-Freez.*

KNEES: Big black limo pulls up, OK? Driver gets out. Huge guy. Big as a horse. Comes in, orders two ice cream cones. I'm sitting right here. Johnny's behind the counter. Driver says, you know who I got back there in that limo? Marilyn Monroe and Jackie Gleason. I walked out there. Thought maybe I could get her to autograph my dick or something. I don't know what I thought. I just wanted to see her. But the windows were all dark. I couldn't see through the glass. It was dark glass. I couldn't see nothing through it. I was standing two feet from Marilyn Monroe. And there was just this dark glass separating us. I could have reached out and touched her. The hell of it is, I'll never be sure. I'll never know absolutely for sure if I was really that close to her or not. My whole life is like that. I mean with women. It's like with the teacher. The girl who got fired. I was just getting to feel like her and me was, maybe, you know, slowly, kind of, establishing some sort of a relationship, you know? She used to smile at me so sweet. In her little yellow sundress. I think she was really getting to like me. I mean, you know, to get past the way I look, which is not necessarily, at first glance, all that impressive. She got fired for screwing some guy in the coatroom after school. Her fiancé from Nebraska or some damned thing. It just makes me mad, you know? I just start to make a friend, and now she's gone. She moved out. She moved back to Wichita or some damned place. I don't even know where she went. One minute she's there, and the next minute she's gone, and you can't ever get to her again. It's just like Marilyn. She's right there, but she's behind the fucking glass. I can't see her, and I can't touch her. That's what it's like with women. It's like a fucking torture chamber. You're so close, but you can't touch them. You think maybe they like you, but you don't know for sure, and you don't want to touch them, in case they don't want you to touch them, but maybe they want you to touch them, but you're the guy, so you're supposed to make the move, and I never know whether I should make the move or not, and by the time you decide you should make the move, they're gone, or they're eating ice cream in a limo with some damned fat son of a bitch like Jackie Fucking Gleason. It's like the time I met this really nice girl in a bar, and we was actually starting to hit it off, really talking, you know? And then I went up to the bar to get us a couple of beers, and this big-ass damned bartender looks down over the bar at me and he says, Hey, buddy, are you really that short, or are you standing on your knees? And the girl laughs, and everybody in the bar laughs, and they start calling me Knees, and now everybody in Phoenix calls me Knees. It's like I'm a fucking walking joke. And then you walk into the damned coatroom, and there's the nicest girl you ever met, being fucked like a dog by some shit kicker from Nebraska. It's enough to make a person want to shoot himself in the fucking head.

# ON AN AVERAGE DAY
John Kolvenbach

Dramatic
Bobby, twenties

*Bobby is a more than slightly crazy fellow who lives physically in the home of his dead parents but who really lives pretty much in his own mind. Recently, while hitchhiking, a guy picked him up and offered him twenty dollars (to do what?), and here he tells his older brother Jack how he reacted. By the way, Bobby is awaiting trial for murdering this man.*

BOBBY: I didn't Care what he wanted, Jack. I was . . . I was *desperate* to transact with the guy. For some reason? Even with the world's *worst* guy sitting there, all I wanted (I couldn't *help* it, like I caught a *disease*) I was suddenly *Aching* to *Transact* with this man. *(Pause. Quietly, and with a kind of amazement.)* He takes out his Wallet. (He's smiling at me like we're in on something.) He takes out his Wallet, this loaf of *bread,* this Loaf, and he pulls out a Twenty. *(Beat, then wondrously.)* A twenty-dollar bill. He holds it up, up by his face (he's *grinning*) and I'm Transfixed by the thing. I'm Mesmerized by the bill, Jack, and Suddenly: He's holding a *treat.* He's holding a *snack,* he's a big *kid* and I'm his *dog,* But now he's a fat *child* holding a *hammer* and I'm *panting,* I'm *salivating,* staring up at the thing: Will I Roll Over? Will I *Heel?* Will I Do Him This *Kindness? (Beat.)* It's not Transacting now, Jackson. You wanna know what it is now? Honestly? I want him *Gone.* All I want in the world is for the fat child to go away. I reach out for the twenty, but I go right past it. I Open his Door. *(Beat.)* We're doing fifty, *easily,* and his door is wide Open. *(Beat.)* The guy doesn't *react.* He's holding the twenty, up in the air, still smiling at me, like am I gonna Fetch, but his *door* is wide *open,* like he hasn't had an *instinct* since *birth,* like he pays somebody to *wipe* him, Jack. I reach under his legs. *(Beat.)* Both hands, I touch his Ass and his Legs and I tip him out. I tip him over, out the open door. He's light. There's no sound. *(Beat.)* Like he gets sucked up the Chimney. Blank. He just all of a sudden isn't there anymore.

# ON AN AVERAGE DAY
John Kolvenbach

Dramatic
Jack, thirties

> *Jack and Bobby are brothers, abandoned by their father years ago. When they were kids, Jack used to tell Bobby stories, fantasies about their father. Jack, in turn, abandoned Bobby; but he has come back after eighteen years and here tells him the truth about their father.*

JACK: What are you now, Bob? Are you a child now? *(Pause.)* You wanna hear a Story? You wanna hear a True one? *(Pause.)* Couple of kids get home from school one day. It's raining. They're stuck inside, passing time. They wrestle, they fight. The little one cries, the big one says he's sorry, couple hundred games of crazy eights. They're waiting for their Father to get home. *(Beat.)* After a hundred years, it's five-fifteen. His car pulls into the driveway. The little one runs to the window, sticks his forehead on the glass. The older one is fourteen, you'd think he wouldn't, but he can't help himself: He stands next to his brother, looking out. *(Beat.)* But the father doesn't get out of the car. It's five-thirty. He's watching the fog creep up the inside of the windshield. It's six, he's parked in his driveway. Six-thirty. He does this some nights. It's seven o'clock. (I Know what he's doing, Bob. He's making a promise to himself, again and again: I promise not to start the car, not to back out onto the road, not to drive away.) Another hour passes. The keys are in the ignition. (All you have to do is turn it, is all it takes, it's all you have to do.) He touches the keys. He tastes a little puke at the back of his throat. *(Beat.)* He gets out of the car. *(Beat.)* The kids come into the kitchen (they come in here) to find him sitting at the table, eating. He's got a piece of bread and a glass of water. The boys stand side by side, near the stove and they watch him. The sound of them watching presses on the back of his neck, and he wonders which one is the German shepherd, which one is the guard. He decides the older one is handcuffs and maybe the other one is more like a rotting mattress. *(Beat.)* But the boys, though, the boys are mesmerized. They watch him chew. They watch him swallow. Drink water from his glass. He's fascinating. This is how it's been, for as long as they've been alive, and still, they Gape at the father eating: Maybe this time he'll melt, maybe he'll turn to glass, or turn around, or choke, or maybe this time he'll speak to us. *(Beat.)* Then the father stands. The boys know their signal. They hurry off to bed. They lie under the covers thinking about tomorrow, thinking: maybe tomorrow. *(Beat.)* The next morning, the younger one wakes up early. You wake up to pee. You come back, you stand by my bed, breathing. *(Pause.)* You say, "Where's Daddy?" *(Pause.)* On an average day, he left us. That's who your father is.

# THE ONES THAT FLUT⁊

## Sylvia Reed

Dramatic
Hunter, twenties

> *Hunter was a convict on death row who wrote this letter to Julie Ray Haynes before he was executed. In the play, it is spoken by Hunter. He is trying to make Julie Ray see the goodness in her father, the warden who supervised his execution, from whom she is estranged.*

HUNTER: "I have seen the burden God has laid on men. He has made everything beautiful in its time. He has also set eternity in the hearts of men; yet they cannot fathom what God has done from beginning to end. I know there is nothing better for men than to be happy and do good while they live. That everyone may eat and drink, and find satisfaction in all his toil — this is the gift of God." Ecclesiastes 3:10-13.

Dear Ms. Haynes, You have seen the humanity in me and everyone else in here at the Walls. You have looked into the eyes of people who have killed, men who have done unspeakable things to their fellow man, and you have unearthed their humanity, an archaeologist of the soul uncovering the goodness that has been buried. We thank you for that. But what of your own? You see our humanity and yet you can't find it in your own father. Ms. Haynes, I want you to know that I have asked Warden Haynes to take a stand, to not be a participant in my state-sanctioned murder. I write this not knowing if he will accept my challenge, but also knowing whether he does or not, he is a good man. A beautiful man. A man, who at his very core, has lived his life well and has merely always done what others have expected of him.

I have to believe

That nothing can stop a beating heart.

If not, why do we live?

For the heart will flutter in the absence of the body.

It will beat in the walls of a house,

In the minds of those left behind,

Or in the field on the edge of the conscience.

# PERFECT HARMONY
Andrew Gross and The Essentials

Dramatic
Lassiter, seventeen

> *Lassiter A. Jayson III is the pitch of The Acafellas, a high-school, a cap-pella powerhouse and seventeen-time national champions. Although Lassiter's conducting and arrangements have helped the group win na-tionals every year he's been in high school, he's begun to suspect that per-haps there's something more to singing than just winning competitions.*

LASSITER A. JAYSON III: *(To audience.)* MTV2 is OK, but as pitch, my goal — my dream — is to take us to the next level. Beyond winning. Last night, my parents took me to the Philharmonic to hear them play Beethoven's Ninth with his original metronome markings, and when I heard it, everything became clear. And at first, we're just sitting there and I thought oh fine this piece is pretty enough. But then in the fourth move-ment, I heard it. This buzz. *Whaaaa. Whaaaa.* The contrabassoon. It's the worst instrument ever. *Whaaaaaa. Whaaaa.* It's like this dying duck contaminating the sound. And I wanted to go up there and like wring its neck to end the pain. I tried to plug my ears, but it kept coming through, *whaaaa.* And that's when I heard them. The words. I mean I had heard the words all along, but I don't speak German. I heard the words beneath the music. The truth. It's like without the contrabassoon, you only hear the pretty, but with the ugliness of that angry duck, you transcend pretty, into beauty, into art, into truth. That's what the bas-soon was, a translator for the hidden truth. And I got up out of my seat, and walked out of the concert and hitchhiked home right then, because I knew. I knew I had to show the guys what the power of music really is. The power of music is everything, it's love and hate, and war and peace, and hunger and not hunger. God, it's everything. And that's what I have to bring to the group.

# RE-SOURCING
## Laura Shamas

Comic
Daubney Camp, around thirty-five

> *Daubney is the supervisor of a small Arkansas call-center group that was*
> *part of the American company Ameriblaze, whose jobs have just been*
> *outsourced to India. Here, Daubney comes up with an idea of how the*
> *Arkansas workers can get their old jobs back and get revenge against*
> *Ameriblaze.*

DAUBNEY: Wait. Wait! *(A quick beat.)* That's it. You're brilliant, Reece and
Jimmie A. Props to you, dude. Y'all have just come up with our plan of
attack. We're going to get our old jobs back. *(Standing up.)* We are going
stay right here and pretend to be Indian. *(A beat.)* We are going to pretend to be from *India.* The country, as in somewhere near Pakistan.
We're gonna to band together and fool some big fat company — maybe
ole Ameriblasé herself *(Holds up his pink slip.)* — into hirin' us to work
their phone centers. Mister, I'm as churned up as a June twister, and I'm
not going to sit and take this BS. I'm gonna protest! Think of what it'll
do to this town to go through another shutdown. It'll be death. They
closed the railways and the mines last century. Now they're tryin' to slam
us again by closin' this call center? I'm gonna do the American thing and
STOP THEM. We can't let 'em get away with it. Let's PROTEST! See,
here's the beauty of it. We'll . . . we'll . . . *(A pause, then divine inspira-*
*tion.)* hire someone who is Indian American to act as our front man! He
goes to Houston and sweet-talks Hodson, tells her we're in Bangalore.
They ain't gonna fly out to Bangalore to check on the facilities. Trust me.
They're too cheap for that. They'll take us based on his pitch, and some
dummied photos of a call center. Whatever. They'll never actually see us.
This guy agrees to keep our secret, somehow, for some reason, I dunno
why — prolly money — we'll work that out later. And then we won't
need new jobs! We can stay here and keep our lives same as before as we
PROTEST THIS OUTRAGEOUS ACT OF CORPORATE
FUCKIN' MALFEASANCE. And voilà, we've pulled off the ultimate
twenty-first century corporate revenge shaft plan.

# RE-SOURCING
## Laura Shamas

Seriocomic
Vijay Smith, thirty to forty

> *Vijay, an Indian American, responds to an unusual ad posted on an underground list-serve in Arkansas, seeking someone who has an interest in liberal political book groups and computer programming. At this first encounter, Vijay offers to help the disaffected, out-of-work group with a strange plan to get their outsourced call-center jobs back from India. But is Vijay for real?*

VIJAY: Listen, I'll take the meeting with this woman. But that's it. You're going to have to work out all the other details yourselves. And you'd better make it good. Look, I'm agreeing to this part of it . . . but after that, I'm out. I'm not going to support the exploitation of the culture and people of India. You're going to have to get your own asses in gear for the rest of the plan. You found me in the Arkansas Underground room. I wanted some action. So did you. Let's get the bastards at Ameriblaze! Your plan reminds me of those sixties protests we've all studied in history class, sort of a wired twenty-first century version of a sit-in or something. So I'm down with it. When you think you're ready to execute, call me on my cell from a pay phone. A pay phone. Is someone going to keep track of what I'm about to say? It's procedural and pretty important. Jimmie Alice, can I trust you? You were my initial contact. OK. Keep calling my cell until you reach me. No messages. No e-mail. No faxes. No paper trails. No voice mail. No text messages. Nothing. When I hear your plan, if my identity is not completely protected and/or if I don't like it, I'll bail. So do your homework. I'll need one week's lead time before the trip to Houston. And of course, you're going to have to pay my way to Houston and for my hotel there, as well as expenses. I'll be in disguise, so they won't be able to ID me. And if this EVER, EVER comes out, or gets traced back to me, I'll deny all of it. And, and get — the ACLU to help me press charges against you for — something.

# RUNES
Don Nigro

Dramatic
Arthur, thirty-nine

> *Arthur Wolf is in the midst of an argument with his daughter Vonnie,*
> *sixteen, in his general store in the small town of Armitage, Ohio, in*
> *1898. It's about her mother Evangeline, who has apparently run off.*
> *Vonnie is insisting that her mother would never just abandon them.*
> *Arthur is a difficult man with a prickly personality but has been deeply*
> *in love with his wife; and now, fed up with being misunderstood by his*
> *family, he lashes back at Vonnie.*

ARTHUR: Mother, mother, mother. Always mooning around about your
damned mother. You don't know what the hell your mother would do.
You didn't know your mother. I saved her from the gutter, but did I get
any credit for it? She treated me like some sort of criminal. You've had
enough to eat and a warm place to sleep your whole life because of me.
Do you think that was the first time she ever tried to run off? I've gone
out and drug that woman back here more than once before, when you
kids were little. Because her children needed a mother, even a loony one
like her. At least she knew how to love you when she was here. Children
need at least one parent they can love. I figured, if you couldn't love me,
you could at least love her, so I had to drag her back here. And I think
half the time she only ran off because she liked being drug back. As if it
proved to her I actually cared about her. Although why that should have
mattered to her in the first place I can't imagine. I don't know what the
hell was going on in her head, ever. I was always just guessing. Living
with your mother was like hanging on by your fingernails every second.
You never knew when she was going to step on your hand or what the
hell she was going to do or when she was going to bolt like a deer. But
I told her finally, all right, Evangeline. That's it. You run off again, don't
you expect me to come drag you back here anymore. The next time you
run off is going to be the last time. And it looks like it was. But if you
want to believe I killed her, it's fine with me. I drowned her in Grim
Lake and buried her in the woods out by the Indian caves. Is that what

you wanted to hear? Damned women are so hungry for tragedy they got to manufacture it. I cut her up in little stars and fed her to the hogs. What's the difference if I did? We're all criminals. That gang that runs the bank. Your precious Uncle Harry is crooked as a corkscrew, and his dad before him. Blaine Plum was a crook. August Ballantine. Gus Cornish. All criminals. And it don't stop at the bank. Porky Redding's taken so many bribes he's running out of room in his backyard to bury the money. Do you think there's hooks in hell? Because I could make a lot of money selling the Devil hooks to hang the sinners in this town on. Did I kill your mother? The real question is, why didn't I do it a long time ago?

# RUNES
## Don Nigro

Dramatic
Arthur, thirty-nine

*We are in the small east Ohio town of Armitage in 1898. Arthur Wolf,
a storekeeper, is a private and often difficult man. He is in the midst of
an argument with his very smart but troubled daughter Vonnie, sixteen,
who blames him for her mother's disappearance. Arthur married Evangeline years ago after she was attacked and impregnated by an unknown
person. This child was Nancy, who grew up to love Arthur despite his
prickly personality. But Arthur has never been able to communicate
with either Nancy, or Vonnie, or his son Jonas, who has turned to the
town doctor for a father figure, and he's often been blamed for their
mother's abandonment of the family. Here a very frustrated Arthur finally opens up to Vonnie and tries to make her understand.*

ARTHUR: You don't know what I am. Just being smart don't mean you ain't ig-
norant. You think it's an easy thing to raise a child? You think we're born
knowing what to do? My father died at the Bloody Angle, in the Battle
of the Wilderness. I never got no instruction book on how to be a good
father to my children. Don't mean I didn't try. But trying hard only
seemed to make me worse at it. So you looked elsewhere. Jonas went to
Doc McGort and you to books and your teachers at school. The only
one who never stopped coming to me, looking for a father, hungry for
it, was Nancy, and I wanted to be good to her. You got no idea how
much I wanted to be good to that girl. But every time she got near me,
all I could think about was the obscene violation that made her, that de-
filed your mother forever and took away whatever chance she had to be
a sane and happy person. I know it's not her fault. If I could control how
I feel, life would be a hell of a lot simpler. But everybody's got a crazy
person inside them that don't give a damn what makes sense. Love
makes people crazy. You think I don't know about love? You think I don't
know what it does to a person? I used to hang around this store, when
your grandfather ran it, when I was a boy, just to look at your mother.
I'd walk by here on the way to school every day and hope to see her in
the window, or catch her coming down the steps so I could walk across

the bridge with her. Sometimes I'd see her standing on the bridge, look-ing into the water, so sad. Every day she walked across the bridge, past the mill, to the school, and I followed her like a dog. She knew how I felt. But she was too good for me, then. She only settled for me later, when she was pregnant and desperate. I tried to be good to her, every way I knew how. But the more I tried to please her, the more she'd shrink away from me. Some people can only love what believes it can do with-out us. And all people who really love, love too much. It's always a mis-take to love. Always. But I'll be damned if I can help making it. It's always love that kills you.

# SEDITION
David Wiltse

Dramatic
Megrim, forties to fifties

*Megrim is a government advocate "prosecutor" at a hearing accusing Professor Schrag of sedition for not supporting America's participation in World War I.*

MEGRIM: I couldn't agree more. Nothing is more precious than the freedom of speech — except the freedom of this country. We are here today because of the possibility of sedition. And what is that but the misuse of freedom of speech? Professor, what if you whisper that so-and-so cheats on his exams? What is his recourse against such a rumor? Shouldn't you be held responsible for this slander? Well, a private citizen can confront you or he can sue you. But what if you defame the government? . . . This is a simple business. Some people are saying things that are counter to the war effort. Now, the war effort isn't just one man's opinion — that's what freedom of speech is all about, every man has a right to his opinion — but *war* isn't one man's opinion. War is a national commitment, war requires unity and sacrifice from all of us. Other men might go to war for their king or their emperor, but the United States can't ask you to do that, there is no king. We are a democracy; we go to war for the people, for each other. Only congress can declare war and congress represents all of us, all of us.

If the United States commits itself to war, it's because all of us have jointly said, "Yes, regrettable though it is, the reasons compel us to join hands and fight for one another, for our mutual good, for our mutual safety." That is how things are in a democracy. When a vote is taken and a winner determined, we don't continue to electioneer against him, we don't deny his right to govern, we accept the election, the will of the people prevails. There is great wisdom in that. This country is based on belief in the wisdom of the people. The time for debate is before actions are taken, not after. What shall happen if those who criticize our participation in this war are allowed to rant in bitterness because they're too fearful?

A man at war does not need someone tugging at him, urging him to go home. What would happen if the protestors prevailed? Why, some men would cease to fight, the group would be weakened, the war would be lost. The brave men who died would have died in vain. Can this country — can any country — allow this to happen? Of course not . . . There is a time for freedom of speech — no one is more in favor of that freedom than I — but there is also a time, recognized by wise men, when the freedom to remain silent is more important . . . And so, certain types of speech are not permitted, and rightly so. Those of us safe at home are no less at war than the men fighting for us in the trenches. The effect of that cowardly urging is no less dangerous here than in France. It puts us all in peril.

# SEDITION
David Wiltse

Dramatic
Schrag, forties to fifties

*Professor Schrag is defending himself against his "inquisitor," Megrim,
of a charge of sedition for not supporting America's participation in
World War I.*

SCHRAG: We like to think of it that way, don't we? All of the people casting
their free and independent ballot. But half of the country are women,
and they can't vote. Most of the colored citizens in the southern states
are excluded by property requirements, literacy tests, and simple intim-
idation. What's that, another ten percent? This is a nation of an unend-
ing flow of immigrants; they can't vote. Another ten percent? How many
free and independent voters does that leave us? Thirty percent? But,
sadly, how many of them can be troubled to vote? Two-thirds? Not that
many, but let's say so. That leaves twenty percent, Mr. Megrim. And how
many of those owe a greater allegiance to their church to secure their sal-
vation or to the political machines, the Tammany Halls that buy their
votes for a beer and a free lunch, or the employers who threaten to fire
them? . . . How many cast their ballots automatically for their party af-
filiation unwittingly, as though they were supporting a sporting team?
What have we left? Ten percent who cast a free and independent ballot?
And our candidates are elected with a mere majority of that — or, in
President Wilson's case, less than fifty percent of the vote the first time
. . . This is democracy as it is practiced in this country, Mr. Megrim.
I don't think I have defamed it by defining it, have I?

# SEDITION
David Wiltse

Dramatic
Schrag, forties to fifties

*Professor Schrag is defending himself and the Constitution to Megrim,
his antagonist, against charges of sedition for not supporting America's
part in World War I.*

SCHRAG: Everyone in this country is battling for liberty, Mr. Megrim,
whether they know it or not, but it's not an external enemy that can take
away our liberty; we are always perilously close to doing it to ourselves
. . . because it's so easy to give up. Freedom is heavy, freedom is hard,
freedom is a burden. It would be such a relief to surrender it all to the
tyrants, the church, the state, all the powerful men that would relieve us
of the nuisance and frustration of listening to other people speak their
minds. The men who wrote our constitution cried out for all the world
to hear the incredible statement that we, the people, the common people of the United States of America, had freedoms. Freedom to speak,
freedom to assemble, freedom to worship. There has never been a docu-
ment like it.

All the tablets of scripture, every boss and bully in history, every
priest and politician tells us what we shall not do; only our Bill of Rights
tells us what we are free to do . . . It happened only once, and if it's gone,
it may not be renewable because it is assaulted constantly, fervently, by
those with power who know it is all that stands between them and complete control. Tell a European serf or peasant what to do and he will do
it. He is untroubled by notions of his right to defy his superiors or his
right to have his own opinion about what is to be done — because he
has no such right. But tell an American what to do, and there is something in his character of the teenaged boy rounding to maturity, a stiff-
necked insistence that age and position do not confer wisdom, that his
life is his own and he will live it as he will. Why does an American of
forty or fifty years still feel this way? Because he knows he has the freedom to do so, that it is enshrined in his Constitution, that it, truly, is the
lasting will of his people — the one beacon that persists despite the ex-

citement of the moment, the hysteria, the deceits, the efforts of those meaning well and ill alike to change it, the inadequacies of our voting, the shifting winds of world events . . . Despite all those, there remains that proud, insistent voice within every American that says, "I am free, I am free." The struggle to remain free is the war that all of us are engaged in every day. I support that war, Mr. Megrim. I support that never-ending war.

# SOME MEN
## Terrence McNally

Dramatic
Will, thirties to forties

> *Will is having lunch with his best friend, Bernie. Both men are married, but the topic of discussion is whether or not they are going to have a sexual affair with each other. Bernie is very much for it, but Will has strong reservations about it.*

WILL: Both our wives think we're best friends. If my wife says anything she got from Susan, I'll kill you, Bernie. I will track you down wherever you and some hustler are holed up, and I will kill you with my two bare hands. I'm not going to let you destroy my life because you've decided to destroy yours. It's all this "gay is good" crap out there in the air all of a sudden. Gay is not good. Gay is loneliness and secrecy and a lifetime of shame. Gay sucks, but they don't tell you that. They only tell you the good stuff you have with the twenty-year-old twinkie. They don't tell you about the ostracism, the jokes behind your back at the office. They don't tell you what it does to your career. They don't tell you what it does to your parents. It will kill them, Bernie. They don't tell you what it does to your kids. Do you honestly think they'll ever want to lay eyes on you again when they find out their father is just another faggot cocksucker? I feel sorry for you. Don't come running to me. Don't even come near me ever again. I don't know you after this. We are closed. Waiter! You asshole. You stupid fucking asshole. Waiter!

# SOME MEN
## Terrence McNally

Dramatic
Michael, twenties

> *Michael tells a group of his friends (all gay men) about a strange sexual*
> *encounter he had the night before with a married man in a hotel room,*
> *even though he is getting married next month.*

MICHAEL: Do you want to hear this or don't you? We were in an elevator. He
said hi. Right off I saw he was wearing a wedding band. We had a drink.
He said he was married and straight but fooled around. I'm sure he was
a member in good standing of the Moral Majority. Straight men who
have sex with us usually are.

. . . He said his wife was out of town. Eugene was, too. Actually, he's
still on the West Coast working on that Susan Sarandon/Tim Robbins
project, but I would never bring someone back to our place. I did once,
and it freaked me out. It was our home, and I'd made it a fuck pad.
Never again, I swore.

. . . He asked me to tie him up and fuck him . . . He goes into the
closet, and he's got all this bondage gear hidden away in his gym bag, and
to make a long story short, I've got him tied up, and then he says he has to
be gagged first, too, and so I gag him and he does look kinda sexy still, and
I'm hard, so I fuck him but fast and without much feeling, and when I pull
out, I suddenly feel such a revulsion for him and what I've done that I want
to do something really awful to him. I told him that, too. I said, "I want to
do something terrible to you," and he just nodded and shook his head, like
that is exactly what he wanted me to do. You know what I did? This is what
I did. I took his ring. *(He has the ring in his hand.)* What is marriage? What
does this ring mean? Does this mean he loves her? Can you love someone
and wear a ring and still ask a stranger to come home with you and tie you
up and fuck you? *(He puts the wedding band on his left ring finger.)* Will a
ring mean I love Eugene when we get married next month? Does marriage
mean we don't sleep with other people? I can't stop or maybe I don't want
to, which? I want to be faithful to my partner, and I can't be. *(Sliding the
ring on and off his finger.)* Michael and Eugene, Eugene and Michael.
*(Then.)* I left him there like that, trussed up like a turkey, and told the door-
man that Mr. Martin in fourteen D needed his help ASAP.

# SOMETHING INTANGIBLE
## Bruce Graham

Comic
Tony, thirties to forties

*Tony Wiston is the owner and founder of the first movie studio dedi-
cated to animation. His greatest creation is Petey Pup. In this scene,
a new young artist, Leo Baxter, has brought in a story idea that Tony
doesn't feel is quite right.*

TONY: Leo, Petey is the second most recognized face in the entire world. Any
idea why? Because he's always the same from story to story. Petey Pup is
bigger than you and me — all of us. J. Edgar Hoover himself wears a
Petey Pup watch. *(A deep breath.)* Petey is an institution and you don't
screw around with an institution, OK, Leo?

*(Smiling warmly.)* It's OK, it's OK. You're new. *(Pacing.)* Now. let's
rethink the story.

*(Back to normal.)* I like the venue — the bank. Never done that.
And the pennies, that's gold. Gags for days. Something's not right,
though. There's just . . . I don't know . . . something's missing.

*(He thinks.)* Something's . . . missing. I don't know, Leo. If I did it
wouldn't be missing. It's what we call an intangible.

*(Spinning on Leo.)* Leo, what's a policeman? *(Before he can answer.)*
An authority figure! Petey's not an authority figure — it goes against his
whole character. Authority figures are what Petey has to overcome.
Cranky landlords, mean bosses, big guys sitting in front of him at the
ball game — they are the enemy!

*(Kneeling at Leo's feet almost seductively.)* Leo, Petey is a combination
of Horatio Alger and Harold Lloyd. He overcomes obstacles by pluck
and luck. He is not — and never will be — a cop.

*(Leaping back up.)* Go to screening room A and get Iggy to run
every Petey short we've ever made. Even the silents.

*(Points to Dale.)* Who is he? He's not my brother. He is the audience! If he doesn't buy it, neither will ten million other people. If he so
much as wiggles in his chair —

*(He illustrates.)* — I know something's wrong — something's missing. We don't release anything from this studio without the approval of
my brother's ass.

# SOMETHING INTANGIBLE
Bruce Graham

Comic
Tony, thirties to forties

*Tony Wiston is owner and founder of the first studio dedicated to animation. Here, he explains to his brother and business partner, Dale, his latest innovation in animation for their new film* Sinbad the Sailor.

TONY: For the first time ever we are going to animate . . . a real person. An actual human being.

(*Reading Dale's mind.*) No, Popeye is not a real person. I want them to believe it's a human being up there. And you know how we're gonna do it? We'll shoot a live-action version first! Hire a low-budget Doug Fairbanks. Black and white. Cheap film stock. Rudimentary costumes and sets.

(*Getting excited.*) What we do is let the boys study the motion before they start drawing.

(*Acting it out.*) How does Sinbad move? How many steps does he take? What does he look like when he LEAPS onto the deck of another ship? How do his clothes billow around him when he slashes his sword? Don't say a word, don't say a word. It'll save us a fortune. Instead of tearing up a lot of drawings, the boys'll study it and do it right the first time. (Petey'll be the) first mate and loyal friend.

(*The pace quickens.*) Sinbad's kidnapped in the first reel, and it's up to Petey to rescue him and save the treasure. And the gags — Goldy's in her fishbowl getting tossed back and forth in a storm and she gets seasick and does all these cute faces (*He imitates a goldfish trying not to vomit.*) — while trying not to puke. And Paula will be lady-in-waiting to the human princess that's Sinbad's love interest. It's all there! I thought it up during the second set. Won six-four. So, whatta you think?

# SPARE CHANGE
Mia McCullough

Dramatic
Brad Thompson, thirties

> *Brad works in finance and has suddenly found his life without purpose or meaning. After meeting a young woman on the El who is fleeing an abusive boyfriend, he is acutely aware of how disconnected he is from everything outside his tiny world. He is speaking to his wife.*

BRAD: I thought we had ideals. I thought there was a certain way we wanted to live. Not the white-bread world of our parents, but something different. Don't you remember that conversation we had in college? That was a crystallizing moment in my life, that conversation. We talked about traveling to Africa, Asia, Vietnam, experiencing different cultures, having our eyes open to the world. We were going to join the Peace Corps. But we didn't go anywhere. Maui. And now we live in this tiny little world. Our city is huge, diverse, and we live in this tiny piece of it, up above it all in this high rise, ignoring everything we don't have time for, which is . . . everything, I think. Everything important. And now you want to move to the suburbs. The suburbs!

   . . . Strip malls and mediocrity masquerading as life, as safety. Or that fucking place where Beth and Philip live. A gated community where people walk around, no, I'm sorry: *drive* around, like zombies. Pretending their development is a community when really it's isolation. Is that what you want? Because if that's what you want . . . I didn't sign up for that. That place makes my skin crawl. If we move to a place like that we may as well sell our souls and become Republicans.

   . . . You move out there where everything's white and clean, and you forget. You forget that everybody's not just like you. And then you don't have to care. And I feel like I've *already* forgotten to care, even here, in the middle of everything.

   What happened to us?

# STILL THE RIVER RUNS
Barton Bishop

Dramatic
Wyatt, twenty-five

> *Wyatt is a troubled veteran of the war in Iraq. He is quiet and reserved,*
> *introspective. He has returned to his central Florida hometown for the*
> *funeral of his grandfather (whom he and the family called Paw-Paw).*
> *Wyatt and his brother, Jesse, have secretly stolen their grandfather's body*
> *from the funeral home. Their plan is to carry Paw-Paw across the*
> *Florida landscape to a wildlife refuge, where he will be safe from the*
> *suburban sprawl devouring their hometown. Jesse, having doubts about*
> *the nature of their plan, has pressed the reluctant Wyatt to tell him*
> *whether or not he believes in God.*

WYATT: There's a spirit. That's what I believe. An energy, really's, what it is,
it's . . . *(Pause.)* There is somethin' greater 'n all of us. Not *so* great that
we ain't a part of it. When we're born, it breathes itself into us.

Every time we kiss someone, it, it passes between the two of us.
When we conceive a child, it churns the womb o' the mama. It . . . It
don't think *thoughts,* it just . . . It blows gentlelike across the universe, in-
different to whether or not we covet our neighbors' wives or sleep in on
Sunday or . . . It don't *have* t' care, see, 'cause it just *is.*

Everything just *is.* It don't sit on no throne, strokin' no beard. He
ain't takin' prayer requests. Keepin' lists. Bible says to us God created
man in his image. Me, I think it's the other way around. I figure man
went 'n' created God in *his* image. Judgment. Needin' to be admired.
Wantin' to punish things. Needin' to feel superior. Those are things a
man does. Those are man's needs. Why would somethin' with the power
to perfectly balance the Great Who Knows concern itself with all that
horseshit? It feels us, to be sure.

Hell, when we hurt, I, I imagine it hurts a little, too.

The more hurtin' that goes on, the more it prob'ly hurts.

But it ain't separate from us. It ain't we down here and it up there.
It shimmers in everything we touch. All you gotta do to know God is to
ask the wind where the hell it's off to.

# STILL THE RIVER RUNS
## Barton Bishop

Seriocomic
Jesse, early twenties

> *Jesse and Wyatt have snuck away from the funeral of their grandfather
> with Paw-Paw's body in the back of Jesse's truck. The estranged brothers
> have been driving through a tense and awkward silence, which Jesse fi-
> nally decides to break.*

JESSE: Ya' shouldn't o' opened your mouth 'bout Joleen. *(Pause.)* That there's
an ugly history. 'N' it's best left as that. History. *(Pause.)* 'Sides, ya
didn't mean what you said. *(Pause.)* I figure if ya don't mean what you're
sayin', why say it? That's what I figure. *(Pause.)* Daddy don't know that.
He spouts idiot wind all the time. But not me. I never say nothin' I don't
mean. Nothin'. And if I do — I preface it. I say — "Now I don't really
mean this, but . . ." so on and so forth. *(Pause. They drive in silence.)* That
wife of Gordon's is somethin' else, ain't she? Kathy? I don't know how he
does it, keepin' up with her. She's like one o' them little windup things,
them little teeth with feet. I'm glad my wife's the shy and silent type.
Easier to . . . *(Long pause.)* I am sure gonna miss the way Paw-Paw'd
make his glass eyeball pop out and roll across the floor like a marble.
That was a real riot. Every time. Never got old. *(Pause.)* 'Member that?
*(Pause.)* I loved that eye. You'd ask him how he lost his eye, different
story every time. *(Pause.)* "Guadalcanal. Goddamn Japs." *(Pause.)* "Tore
it out myself one night 'cause I was sick o' lookin' at your Mee-Maw.
Would torn the other out but I passed out." *(Pause.)* "Bears!" *(Pause.)*
"Cancer!" . . . *(Pause.)* What was the last thing you buried? Last thing I
buried? One o' Cox's cows spit up this little runt of a cow. Looked like
an alien. Killed the mama on the way out. Premature or somethin'. But
I swear, Wyatt, if I didn't know any better? I'd say a pig had its way with
that heifer 'n' that lil' cowpig was the result.

# STILL THE RIVER RUNS
Barton Bishop

Dramatic
Wyatt, twenty-five

> *It is dawn. Jesse and Wyatt, their truck having broken down, have walked all night, carrying their grandfather's body across fields and through swamps. They have finally arrived at the spot where they are going to bury him. Jesse has figured out that Wyatt doesn't have time to report back to Fort Benning on time, so he has asked Wyatt where he's really going once he leaves home again. This is his reply.*

WYATT: Ya know that ratty ol' Desert Inn out near Yeehaw Junction? Girl by the name o' Maria tends bar at that dusty ol' joint downstairs . . . What I'm gonna do, Jess . . . I'm gonna hitch my way to Yeehaw Junction. Told Maria a couple o' years back I'd be comin' 'round again. She and I, we had a tussle in one o' the original brothel rooms . . . Her lips, I swear, they came to mine like cool, crisp water would come to my mouth Over There. Petrichor. *(Pause.)* Dippin' into that woman was like reachin' into the cookie jar, I tell you what . . . *(Pause.)* I'm gonna stroll into that bar. Have me some drinks. Have me a *lot* o' drinks.

*(Long pause.)* I don't got a favorite memory, but I got a favorite place. Balcony o' that rat-dung hotel. At that Junction — Four-forty one, state road sixty. Not balcony, really, ya' just set up a chair outside o' your door. Round about seven o'clock. Crack open a Natty Light 'n' a bottle o' Jim Bean, 'n' watch them sunbeams reach down through the afternoon clouds. Like God's fingers stretchin' out to caress those boundless, glorious plains that never stop rollin'. At least not that a fella can see from where he's sittin'.

*(Pause.)* 'N' when the sun goes down, I'm just gonna go inside 'n' keep drinkin. Drinkin' 'n' drinkin' . . . 'Til there ain't no beat in my heart. *(Pause.)* They'll come lookin' for me, Jesse. Tell 'em they'll find me at those crossroads. I'll be in an upstairs room. I'll be as still as the waters o' Lake Toho at dusk.

# STRETCH
## Susan Bernfield

Dramatic
The Orderly, about nineteen; former grade-school shrimp

*The Orderly is speaking to his childhood friend with whom he hangs out and smokes pot every day after work. He has grown up in a small town, without much hope or guidance for the future. He has a dead-end job in a nursing home, but he's finding he likes the work. He's begun to respect the old people in the home, and he likes feeling that he can be of use. He's begun to connect the stories he hears from the old folks with the lack of a purpose in his own life. He's beginning to discover that he may want to make something of himself.*

ORDERLY: I'm in the medical profession, man, it's a profession . . . *(Beat.)*
    I don't mind. I mean, I do, but . . . it's not just that, man.
    I dunno, these old people, these old people, right? Some of 'em are fucked up, but I like 'em, y'know. I like helping 'em. I know it's just a job, man, but I dunno, they — they had lives, y'know. With jobs and insurance and houses an' shit. Like normal people, and now they're normal old. What's that anymore, man? You know anybody does that? Everybody hates their parents.
        Goes out and tweaks.
        Blows up their house.
        All these houses, half the town, blowing up . . .
        Dudes up and joining the army.
        'cause your house could blow up or *you* could, OK,
        *(He laughs.)*
        so what's the difference
        by the side of some road in some far-off craziness place
        or get to the emergency room all burnt and in shreds, OK
        rather clean up some old guy's pee.
        Listen to his crazy stories.
        Try ta get some kinda clue
        how people s'pposed ta be.

# THERE OR HERE
Jennifer Maisel

Dramatic
Ajay, thirties

*Ajay, unable to sleep while his wife is in the hospital, has driven from New York City to the town he grew up in on Long Island. He is at the drive-through of the fast-food restaurant where he worked in high school.*

AJAY: I used to work at this drive-through, you know. In high school. They didn't have the Pan Asian beef salad when I worked here. Then they were strictly patriotic cuisine, none of the cross-cultural dining experience you're blessing the public with now. I used to eat a double cheeseburger, no sauce, extra pickles, fries, onion rings, chocolate shake on my break every time I came to work. I loved this job. I loved my free meal that wasn't the kind of food my mom cooked at home. I loved the french-fry polyester smell of the uniform. I'd put the onion rings and the fries in the sandwich which I thought was genius, very American of me — gave me that super-American fast-food breath. I was probably one of the three kids "of color" in my high school class, and I didn't really count as an "of color" except for the fact it made them feel more multicultural, which was a word that was just coming into style. There were two black kids . . . and me.

I liked the anonymity of working the window here — I liked that folks would hear my voice and picture me one thing and then pull up for their burgers and shakes and surprise! — no Aryan linebacker filling their order — just me — double surprise — I was the linebacker too. I live in the city now. And I woke up, and my wife isn't there because she sent me home from the hospital to get a good night's sleep, and I thought I would, you know, because she wasn't there, but I couldn't . . . And I needed to go somewhere, bust the fuck out, and I drove out here to my old house . . . the people who live there, it doesn't look the same, and I drove past the school and didn't recognize it. And I thought at least I could smell something that's the way it used to be, taste something that's the way it used to be, and now you tell me that the fucking Pan Asian beef salad is very popular.

I can't think of another place to go . . . I used to wonder whether they put me at the drive-through because I was good at it or because they didn't quite know what to do with my face. Does that ever occur to you? But I did have friends, you know, friends who didn't think twice, so I think that was just me. If I came in? If I came in and sat down at the corner table and got my food at the counter where I used to sit on my breaks, do you think you could come out and say hi? Jessica?

# THREE CHANGES
Nicky Silver


Dramatic
Hal, forties

> *Hal, a writer, is telling his brother about how he lost everything and now is destitute.*

HAL: It's true, Nate. I did. I got everything I wanted. And now it's gone. I made shit, Nathan. Mountains of shit, mountains of it. It gets in your eyes and in your nose and everything smells terrible. And then one day you realize that odor is you. And the joke is, the hilarious and terrible joke, is that I wasn't even good at it. I knew it. They knew it. The twenty-year-old motherfucker piece of shit who covered for me knew it. I couldn't come back, all these years, I couldn't, because I was high. So fucking high I couldn't drive, or think, or leave my house. I burned down my bedroom and spent my mornings vomiting. I shit in my pants. But I was working and I was someone . . . and then it ended and I disappeared. And now it's gone. All that money. In my veins and up hustlers' asses. It was fun. That's the truth. Some of it was fun. But I had no idea exactly how much I wanted to die. And I found myself, one morning, in a park, in soiled clothes, on the grass, tasting puke in my mouth . . . And I gave up. I just gave up. I told the sky, or God, or the dirt, or the grass that it was too much, all too much. It was time. So I let someone or something take over my life. And He did. God did. Jesus did. I couldn't run it any more, my life. I couldn't. And He saved me. . . . I got out of rehab two weeks ago. There's nothing left. No home. No money. Nothing. So I called you. Did I do the wrong thing?

# THREE ON A COUCH
Carl Djerassi

Dramatic
Stephen, fifty

> *Stephen Marx, a famous New York novelist, has staged his death in a*
> *fake sailing accident. He is obsessed by the idea of reading his own obit-*
> *uaries and then taking on a new identity (initially under the name of*
> *T. H. Lustig), writing and working under different heteronyms. Only*
> *his former therapist knows that he is still alive. This is Marx's rational-*
> *ization in response to the therapist's questions.*

STEPHEN: The public loves a tragic death. The only one losing out is my former editor. He'll have to find himself some new talent. Most of the time,
I feel freer than I have in years. But you're right: there are days when I
crave some company. Communing solely with my heteronyms . . . real
as they seem . . . doesn't make up for . . . what shall I call it . . . the fris-
son of truly human engagement? But I do compensate in other ways.
I've even taken up cooking. Last night I had red snapper . . . in a white
wine sauce. With grilled asparagus. Little fat . . . not too many calories
. . . I'm becoming a true Californian. Marx went to California, but
Lustig now lives in upstate New York . . . three hours away from you
. . . by car . . . and an old one at that. Initially, I went to California for
my Social Security number and a cell phone. I like their food and the
fact that Californians don't smoke . . . but that's about it. Earthquakes
make me nervous. Besides, New York isn't just Manhattan . . . upstate
there's some spectacular countryside and plenty of privacy. Impressed?

# THE TUTOR
## Allan Havis

Dramatic
Orson, sixteen.

*Orson Bentley visits his family tutor, Seth Kane, in Kane's hospital room. Kane is in a coma, and Orson delivers a semidelusional monologue of contrition.*

ORSON: Hello, Mr. Kane. It's Orson. I'm dreadfully sorry for you. *(Pause.)* I know you can't speak, and the nurse said I could only stay for a few minutes. I brought you roses. Pink roses. I guess we need a vase and some water. *(Pause.)* I know you you're in a coma, and I found myself praying every night to God to keep you alive. I felt that God was hearing me out, and there was never a real busy signal on the line. I tell kids at school that I believe in God now. I think I will get to church and light a candle to show my supplication. *(Pause.)* I aced my English lit final. Got the second highest score in the class. Thanks to you, Mr. Kane. Really. Some things are pure magic. *(Pause.)* Can't you talk just a little? *(Pause.)* My mom and dad were really upset to hear what happened to you. Dad really showed emotion. And you could see a few tears welling up in his eye. *(Pause.)* Tucker stole my snake, Mr. Kane. He had my house key and the alarm code. I thought he would never take my pet. He knew my snake was my best friend. He killed my snake. *(Pause.)* Everyone underestimates Tucker because people think I'm the killer. I wouldn't harm a fly. My mother taught me to hold back from that sort of thing. I thought Tucker would only do stunts to scare me. Because I taught him everything I know, and he picked up everything like a sponge. But *he* put the fucking rattler inside your car. I don't own a rattler. That motherfucker bought a rattler in TJ. Now Tucker knows how bad this turned out. He's like Ed Norton in *Primary Fear*. You know, like Jeckle and Hyde. Fooling even the Devil. *(Pause.)* The nurse said you had complications from rhabdomyolysis. Man, that is so out. Rattlers never bothered Eve. Never bothered Adam. They only bothered God's angels. And really I am to blame for all of your pain. When I really should say something I feel in my heart. I love you, Mr. Kane. I love you. I love you. I love you. And fucking Tucker was so jealous of you that it had to come to this. I was lying sometimes, but you knew when I was honest. I love you like a father, Mr. Kane. I really love you. I'm so ashamed of how things turned out. And I'm afraid that I've lost you. A boy needs a father. I need to be bleached clean, Mr. Kane. Please don't abandon me. I beg you. I would even die for you and burn in hell. Please give me a chance?

# TWO THIRDS HOME
## Padraic Lillis

Dramatic
Michael, thirty-one

> *Michael is addressing Sue, his mother's lover of seventeen years, on the
> day of his mother's funeral. Sue has criticized Michael of being too self-
> ish to acknowledge the loss that she is experiencing and that the rela-
> tionship between her and his mother is something Michael has never
> tried to or will never understand.*

MICHAEL: Do you think I'm an idiot? I didn't try to understand it because she
did everything she could to tell me not to. You slept in her room, and
she never acknowledged it. The door just got locked one day — I'm
sorry if I don't share how she felt about you. I never saw it. But I knew
it was something not to talk about. So, I didn't say anything. To my
neighbors, friends, family. Nobody. But don't think I didn't understand.
I knew her. She told me everything — but not about you. And now I'm
thirty-one years old, I got a kid, and I stood in front of a church today,
and I didn't know what to say. And more than anything, I'm ashamed of
that. I loved her — but I didn't know what I was allowed to tell people.
I knew not to talk about you. I knew not to invite people back to the
house. I don't even know if she'd want me in this house today. I know
she'd want you here. I know she'd want Paul here. But I don't know
where I belong. And that's your fault. You agreed to it. You let it be a secret. And now that she's gone, no one can share it with you . . . Do you
know what the last thing my mother told me was? It was in the hospital. The last day, when Paul was on the train — and you were asleep in
the chair. She turns to me and says, she says, "I got to go to the bathroom." And so I go to get her bedpan, but she asks if I'll carry her. She
says to me, in this soft voice. You know what I'm talking about. She can
barely whisper. Well, she says, "If I'm going to die in this bed, I'd at least
like the sheets to be clean." So, I go and I pick her up. And as I carry her
to the bathroom, she looks up at me and says, "Make sure Christopher
knows I'm OK. And that I love him. And next year for his birthday I

want you to give him a new bike. From me. OK? He's ready for a two-wheel one now." And I'm telling her not to worry about it. I'm trying to get her into the bathroom before I have to change my shirt. You know? But she keeps going. "And if I don't see Paul, make sure you tell him, I'm proud of him. And make sure the house is taken care of. I don't want Sue to have to deal with anything." And I say, I will. And I sit her down and balance her on the seat. And she looks at me and says, "You can close the door, I'll take it from here."

# A VERY, VERY SHORT PLAY

## Jacquelyn Reingold

Comic
Roger, twenty-five to forty

*Roger is chatting up a woman sitting next to him on an airplane. He doesn't know her. He wishes he did.*

ROGER: I'm sorry to ask, you look so content so calm so reasonably relaxed I'm sorry to ask. Your wrist is just so, and your shoes are just right, what are they pumps, mules, puels? I'm sorry to ask, but that shaft of light is hitting your hair and making it glow. And I know, I do, look at me not exactly coiffed, 'cause this crazy way of getting from here to there makes me well want to die, with its clouds and oh God the sky, I can't help it I'll stop, the rhyming I'll drop. But the question's still in here: I'd love to know yet I hate to ask, but you, you are the smallest woman I've ever seen. So in between the pretzels and the plastic cup of cola, while we're madly flying over Massapequa toward Madagascar, with Anawanda on the right and Alabama on the left, I am compelled while I eat my salted nuts, and if you don't mind, it's a nervousness of mine, take out my hibachi and grill shrimp kebobs: just how tall or small are you, and how delicate are your ankles when they're undressed, and what, if I dare ask, is your name?

# THE VOWS OF PENELOPE CORELLI

Richard Vetere

Seriocomic
Charlie Sunshine, thirties

*Charlie is a not very talented lounge singer, but he has a dream. He is
speaking to Penelope Corelli about her daughter, Sheila Marie, and how
much he cares for her and how special he has found her to be despite the
fact that he only started dating her because Penelope hit the lottery for
fifty-three million.*

CHARLIE: I'm hopin' Sheila Marie has patience for me. I gotta tell you something, Mrs. Corelli. That daughter of yours, she's special. She is. And I'm
torn here. I know you're thinking this only has to do with money, and
even though it does, a little, there are other things in play here that figure into the grand scheme of things that have nothing to do with that
kind of currency. Your daughter is wonderful. That means full of wonder. I mean, what she knows about external dynamics like storm clouds,
Bermuda highs, and humidity is impressive. How many people can you
say know that much about a thing? I can't count more than a handful.
Sinatra knew how to get every emotion a man could feel out of single
lyric. Nelson Riddle knew how to make a beat swing, and Count Basie
knew tempo like Eskimos know snow. And I put Sheila Maria right up
there. I know you don't think there's an ounce of originality in this guy
standing here in front of you, but there is more than you expect. Take
my name for instance, Charlie Sunshine. I made that up for myself.
Yeah! My real name, and this is not for public consumption, is Vincenzo
Calamarie. Yeah, exactly. I thought something like Vinny Cal or
Vin Marie. But then it hit me, what do people look forward to every
morning? Sunshine, right? And what name just rolls off the tongue like
a melting ice cube? Ch . . . ar . . . lie. Charlie Sunshine. See? I got
thoughts. Deep ones. But nothing like your daughter has. I know you
are a woman of exceptional fortitude and personality, but that little girl
of yours, has something neither one of us has, and that is high aptitude.
The kind that don't come along much and when it does, it makes you

see things like you never looked at them before. Like when you check out a cloud and see a face or a mountain range. That's her. The thrill of an exciting imagination rolled up in one hot little body. No disrespect. But you know what I mean. I owe my quick rise in IQ to Sheila Maria. But tragically, I have a dream to pursue. I said my piece, Mrs. Corelli, so as tough it as it is, I must say good-bye and good luck.

# WHERE WE'RE BORN
Lucy Thurber

Dramatic
Drew, twenties

*Drew is a hanger-on type with a fatalistic touch of the poet. He spends a lot of time at his friend Tony's house. Here he tells Franky, Tony's girl-friend, about a walk he recently took, during which he considered setting fire to a church.*

DREW: . . . Nice day out. I've been wandering. I took a walk up Suicide Hill. . . . I hung around up there for a while. You know at night you can see as far as Holyoke, sometimes Springfield. I stayed up there. Then I came down.

. . . I stopped at Charlie's for a few. Played some pool and shit. You know. Then I took a little walk down Upper Russell Road. I walked for a while. I got as far as my father's church. You know the one.

. . . I did a lot of walking. It's good to walk sometimes, don't you think? I mean distance can be a mental thing. You just decide something and then there you are. If a decision is strong enough, it can take you anywhere. That's the problem with decisions. Y'know you can make them casually, like getting dressed in the morning, forget you made them and then blam, there they are, staring you in the face. I got pretty angry today, looking at that church, Frank. I thought about burning it down. I'd start the fire early Sunday morning. So when they all pulled up, y'know, to get their weekly taste of God, the church would be burning, almost all burned up. What do ya think they'd do then? It would be pretty funny to see the look on their faces, don't you think? Where would they go to believe? They'd have nowhere to go, except their homes. People never believe in their homes. They get all dressed up for God, do their hair and shit. Not in their homes though; they're too busy trying to fuck somebody else's wife or girlfriend. You know, Frank, people around here, they're just bored and bored people ain't nice people, Frank.

. . . Sometimes the things we try to believe in lead us further into believing in nothing at all. Sometimes the prettiest things in the world are flat-out poison.

# YEAR ZERO
## Michael Golamco

Dramatic
Vuthy (pronounced "Woo-tee"), sixteen

> *Vuthy, a troubled Cambodian-American teenager, recounts a classic folktale as he asks for help. He's talking to a small human skull that represents the afterlife, death, the spirit world.*

VUTHY: I got a favor to ask you. And I know I been asking you for a lot, and I'm sorry, but I guess I'm the kinda guy that needs a lotta help.

*(Beat.)* So: There's this story that my ma used to tell me. About this great king who left his country, his peoples, because he wanted to learn how to do magic. So that when there was a drought, he could be a rainmaker. And when there was a famine, he could make fruit fall outta the trees. And so he traveled to this foreign kingdom where there was this great wizard, this teacher. And the wizard taught him how to make rain fall outta the sky, and fruit fall outta the trees. And the wizard taught the king how to transform into all sorts of animals, real and mythical. And when he had learned everything he could learn, the king started on his journey back to his people. But he got lost in this huge forest. He wandered for days, began to starve, wondered if he'd ever see his home, his peoples again. But then he had an idea. He would use his magic to turn into a tiger and catch something to eat. So he spoke the right spell and his body transformed — fangs, claws like razors. And he felt more powerful, more majestic than he had ever felt as a king. And he was easily able to catch a stag, and he tore into it with his teeth. And it was an easy thing to catch the next one, and the next one. And he loved life as a tiger — he began to forget that he was ever human — that he was ever a king. And those memories, of his people and his country, turned into a distant dream. This had always been his life. And sometimes he would sleep and dream of being a man. But when he woke up, he knew that he had always been a tiger. And he always would be.

# SCENES

# ALIENS WITH EXTRAORDINARY SKILLS

Saviana Stanescu

Comic
Borat, early thirties
Lupita, late twenties

*Lupita, a Dominican American and an aspiring actress, works as an exotic dancer at strip club in New York City. Borat, an illegal immigrant from Russia, is watching her perform a pole dance at the club. Borat likes Lupita and tries to get a date with her, but his lies about his situation don't help.*

*(Lupita is dancing around a pole for Borat, who's sitting in a comfortable chair, sipping vodka.)*

BORAT: Yeah, baby . . . Yeah.

LUPITA: Whadda you say you do, honey?

BORAT: I'm a . . . doctor.

LUPITA: Oh, yeah. What's your name, doctor? Where are you from, doctor?

BORAT: Steve. Steve from Tennessee.

LUPITA: C'mon, where are you really from?

BORAT: What do you mean?

LUPITA: Oh, yeah. What do I mean. I mean I don't care, Steve. Here you can be whoever you wanna be.

BORAT: *(She makes some very sexy moves.)* Oh, God. What are you doing?

LUPITA: I start from the top and I weeee my way down . . .

BORAT: Wow.

LUPITA: Do you like that, honey?

BORAT: God, yes I'm not sorry for the fifty bucks.

LUPITA: You were worried you paid too much, doctor?

BORAT: No, fifty dollars is nothing for me. I mean . . . I don't mean to offend you . . . I'm rich. I'm very rich. I'm Donald Trump of . . . horse doctors.

LUPITA: Oh, yeah? Horse doctor? I like horses. Great to meet you, "Donald."

BORAT: Horses are good, how do you say, reliable, horses are reliable animals. I help them. Yes, I'm a good horse doctor. Ay, that was nice. Do it again. Ride me, baby, ride me.

LUPITA: "Horse doctor" . . . You're not a Russian spy, are you?

BORAT: Why do you say that? I'm not Russian.

LUPITA: I know accents. I'm an actress. But don't worry, honey, *(Musically.)* here you can be whoever you wanna be, Steve-from-Tennessee.

BORAT: You are smart for a pro . . . professional actress, I mean.

LUPITA: *(Stops dancing.)* I'm not a whore, vodka-boy. Stick that into your mind.

BORAT: Please don't stop.

LUPITA: I'm done. That's what you get for fifty bucks, honey.

*(Borat closes his eyes and puts a hand on his crotch.)*

LUPITA: What are you doing?

BORAT: I'm going to rub my penis to the good memories of you dancing.

LUPITA: Are you crazy? You can't jerk off here. Go to the bathroom. Open your eyes and go to the fucking bathroom.

BORAT: *(With his eyes closed, his hands up to show her he's not touching himself.)* OK, I'm going to imagine that I rub my penis to the good memories of you dancing.

LUPITA: I forbid you to imagine anything about me.

BORAT: You can't do that. The dance was yours, the good memories are mine.

LUPITA: Open your eyes.

BORAT: *(With his eyes closed.)* Wow, that was nice. Do it again.

LUPITA: Loco.

BORAT: *(With his eyes closed.)* Hmmm . . . You are beautiful, mamacita, you damn are.

LUPITA: OK. How do you say "whatever" in Russian?

BORAT: *Ja t'bia ublu. ("I love you" in Russian.)*

LUPITA: I'm done here. *(She's ready to exit.)*

BORAT: *(Opening his eyes.)* Wait, I lied. I'm not a horse doctor.

LUPITA: Whatever.

BORAT: I'm a cab driver.

LUPITA: *(Mockingly.)* Great.

*(She's not really upset but intrigued by the guy. He's quite different from the usual clients. He's kind of fun, in a weird way, of course.)*

BORAT: Can I drive you home after work?

LUPITA: Nope.

BORAT: Tomorrow?

LUPITA: No.

BORAT: On weekend?

LUPITA: How do you say "never" in Russian?

*(She exits, smiling, like "I can't believe this guy.")*

# AND THE WINNER IS
## Mitch Albom

Comic
Seamus, sixties to seventies, but could be any age.
Tyler, forties

> *Actor Tyler Johnes has arrived in purgatory (which looks rather like a traditional Irish pub) the night before his star turn at the Oscars. The barkeep in purgatory, Seamus, is having a hard time convincing the egomaniacal Tyler that he is indeed dead.*

SEAMUS: I need to tell you something. Some take it better than others. *(Beat.)* I have a feeling you're gonna vomit.

TYLER: What is it, old man? You hard up? If you fix me a drink, I can give you a few bucks —

SEAMUS: *(Pointedly.)* Shut it now, lad! I am not your bloody barkeep. *(Sighing, calming down.)* You died. In your sleep. Your heart attacked you. You came down the hatch and now you're here.

TYLER: *(Playing along.)* Um-hmmm . . . OK. So I'm dead.

SEAMUS: Affirmative.

TYLER: And this is where you go when you're dead.

SEAMUS: This is where YOU go.

TYLER: Ah. I see. My eternal rest is a bar with no cigarettes, no phone, and . . . no beer!

SEAMUS: Aye.

TYLER: I can't wait to see where you send Kyle Morgan. I played the *good* cop. *(Chants quickly.)* Ommmm! Ommmm! Come on, old man. A dry bar! Even God can't have that cruel a sense of humor.

SEAMUS: *(Glumly.)* . . . You'd be surprised.

TYLER: Prove it.

SEAMUS: Well, do you remember that little prayer, "Now I lay me down to sleep, I pray the lord my soul to keep"?

TYLER: *(Disinterested.)* Yeah?

SEAMUS: You didn't say it.

TYLER: I didn't say it when?

SEAMUS: The night you croaked. And that's why you're here.

TYLER: I'm here because I didn't say my lines?

SEAMUS: Aye.

TYLER: And where do the lucky people who *did* say it go?

SEAMUS: *(Pointing to window.)* There.

TYLER: The lucky people who say it go to the Oscars?

SEAMUS: Not the Oscars, boyo. Heaven. Valhalla. Shangri La. Abraham's bosom.

TYLER: So this isn't heaven.

SEAMUS: It's . . . a way station.

TYLER: I, I, I, I . . . gotcha.

SEAMUS: Good.

TYLER: NOW can I phone my agent?

SEAMUS: Arrrgh! You're dead, boyo! Don't you get it? There's no phone! Jiminy Peters, you're giving me a headache.

TYLER: You get headaches in heaven?

SEAMUS: Aye.

TYLER: Can you get aspirin?

SEAMUS: I said he has a cruel sense of humor.

TYLER: Right . . . Look, mister. I appreciate this whole charade. It's nice work. Community theater, maybe, but nice work. Now just open the backdoor, and I won't press charges. *(Seamus contemplates something.)*

SEAMUS: I don't like to get physical.

TYLER: *(Laughing.)* What? You're gonna beat me up? OK . . . Bring it on, old man! *(Strikes karate pose.)* I did three karate movies in the eighties! Hyyyyuhh! *(Seamus stares at the silly pose. He gently takes one of Tyler's hands and places it on his chest.)*

SEAMUS: Feel . . . listen . . . *(Tyler goes from confused to slowly panicked. He moves his hand around his chest, then his rib cage. Softly.)* You have no heartbeat . . . because it's not beating anymore . . .

TYLER: *(As it starts to register.)* I . . . died . . . ?

SEAMUS: You took the big dirt nap.

TYLER: No . . . No-ho-ho-ho! . . . *(Rising.)* No! *(Runs in a circle.)* No-no-no-no-no-no-no-no-no NOOOOOOOO! NO-NO-NOOOOOOO!

SEAMUS: I KNEW you wouldn't like it.

TYLER: NOBODY DIES THE NIGHT BEFORE THE OSCARS! YOU MISS ALL THE PARTIES!

SEAMUS: We're not on the same schedule up here.

TYLER: NO-NO-NO-NO-NO! I HAVE A FREAKING LIMOUSINE AT FREAKING FOUR-THIRTY! I HAVE A GIRLFRIEND HALF MY

AGE WITH A LOW-CUT DRESS AND A GREAT ASS THAT I
HAVE BEEN KEEPING FOR JUST THIS OCCASION!

SEAMUS: The dress?

TYLER: THE ASS! *(Starts chanting again, frantically.)* Ommm! Ommmm!
I AM GOING TO THE OSCARS WITH THAT GIRL AND HER
GREAT ASS. OH, YEAH, I AM GOING TO THE OSCARS IF IT
KILLS ME!

SEAMUS: It's a little late for —

TYLER: Don't say it! Don't say another . . . goddamn word.

# BACK BACK BACK
Itamar Moses


Dramatic
Kent, late thirties
Adam, late twenties

> *Teammates for several years early in their baseball careers, Kent and Adam*
> *have not seen each other for about six years. In this scene, they are team-*
> *mates again, if only for a day, on the National League All-Star team. And,*
> *because the all-star game takes place exactly halfway through the baseball*
> *season, Kent is at the halfway point of a run at the single-season home-run*
> *record — a record that, given knowledge Adam has of some extreme mea-*
> *sures Kent took in their younger days, may not actually be legitimate.*

(*It's July 1998 in Colorado. A dugout. Kent is looking out at the field. He is*
*wearing a National League All-Star uniform and a cap.*)

KENT: OK. Come on now. Swing away. Let's see what you got. (*A moment.*
*He applauds.*) That's it. That's what I'm talking about. Yeah. Now. One
more. One more just like that. Come on. (*A moment. He applauds*
*again.*) There it is. There it is. Yeah.
(*Adam has walked up behind Kent. He also wears a National League All-*
*Star uniform and the cap of his new team.*)

ADAM: "You hold that moment till it's over."
(*Kent turns.*)

KENT: What's up, rook!

ADAM: Hey man!
(*Adam goes for the handshake. Kent goes for the hug. They hug awkwardly.*)

KENT: Gosh it's good to see you.

ADAM: I know, right? Too long, too long. Look at you, man! Damn!

KENT: What.

ADAM: You're friggin' huge, man! "Superman" indeed.

KENT: Oh, God, yeah. I was fine with "Kent"? But I guess journalists get
bored easy. (*The cap.*) That's right! You're down South now!

ADAM: Yeah.

KENT: You like it there?

ADAM: (*Shrugs.*) Great team.

KENT: Yeah, man. Great club. Great pitching.

ADAM: Our rotation is indeed fierce.

KENT: Seriously, every time you face those guys, you're happy it's not one guy, turns out it's another guy, Glavine, Maddux, Smoltz —

ADAM: Some of them are here.

KENT: What?

ADAM: Greg and Tommy, they're here. You want to meet them?

KENT: I, uh . . . *(Beat.)* I've met them, Adam. I've been in this thing before.

ADAM: Oh, yeah, no. Right. That's right.

KENT: Yeah. *(Beat.)* That's right! This is your first All-Star Game!

ADAM: Yeah.

KENT: Congratulations, Adam. That is really awesome.

ADAM: Yeah, no, thanks, yeah. He comes up, he breaks in, and ten short years later he makes the National League All-Star Team. It's a really overwhelming story.

KENT: Hey, knock that crap off. You're an All-Star second baseman.

ADAM: Actually they play me in center.

KENT: I, really? *(Beat.)* Point is I never doubted it would happen for you.

ADAM: You don't have to say that.

KENT: Don't listen to me. You're the one got the votes.

ADAM: I, um, I didn't actually, no.

KENT: What?

ADAM: My manager's the National League Team manager, so —

KENT: Right.

ADAM: So he just put me on the team.

KENT: Right, yeah, no, right. *(Beat.)* But! The support of your manager. Who sees you play every day. Over the opinion of some fans who may or may not be even watching, I mean, that's —

ADAM: No. Yes. It's nice to have a manager who believes in me.

KENT: Ahh, fuck Tony. You ever look at his stats from when he played?

ADAM: Well, OK, but managing is a different skill, and that one he's got, I mean, he'll get into the Hall of Fame for managing, so that's not exactly —

KENT: Well, no, I mean, you're right, you're probably right. I'm just saying. *(Beat.)* Or, hey, then maybe look at it that way.

ADAM: What? What.

KENT: That there's a way to have a whole second career. If it doesn't pan out for a guy. As a player.

ADAM: Oh.

KENT: But, no, I mean, hey, don't sell yourself short. Here you are.

ADAM: Here I am. *(Beat. Then, pointing.)* You taking batting practice?

KENT: Did already. Just sticking around to watch. You?

ADAM: Yeah. I'm . . . coming up.

(*A moment.*)

KENT: OK. Bring it on home now. Come on. Bring it on home.

ADAM: *(Simultaneously.)* Swing away. Show it to me. Show me what you got.

(*A moment. They applaud together.*)

KENT: That's what I'm talking about. Nice. Now keep it up.

ADAM: *(Simultaneously.)* Righteous. Cannot argue with that. One more like it.

(*A moment.*)

ADAM: Yeah I always sort of badmouthed it? Meaningless game, empty spectacle, Home Run Derby, souvenir T-shirts. But I gotta say actually being here? Pretty much kicks ass. Especially after such a rough year.

KENT: Right. *(Beat.)* Oh! Hey. My God. Yes. How's your wife?

ADAM: Oh, thanks, she's fine. Thank you. She's doing good.

KENT: Great.

ADAM: She's here actually. She's here to watch the game.

KENT: So she's all recovered.

ADAM: Oh, well, I mean, recovery means different things? The issue now is what impact the whole thing had on her immune system. Like if it's gonna be easier for her to get sick in the future? But, yes, we're OK now as far as the initial scare is concerned, yeah.

KENT: Well you guys seemed to handle it well. I mean, from what I read and saw.

ADAM: Yeah, suddenly the press wanted to talk to me again.

KENT: No, just, I mean —

ADAM: No, yeah, you're right, we hung in there. I mean, we also totally collapsed. Like, after it was over? I don't know. Something like that you sort of put your feelings aside for the duration. But then as soon as there was time, we both just lost it. *(Pause.)* At least out here you know when you're up, right? Out there nobody tells you when those moments are gonna be.

KENT: Well. It's really good that you guys have each other.

ADAM: Definitely. Definitely. *(Beat.)* Oh, God, Kent, yeah. I was really sorry to hear that you split up.

KENT: Oh yeah. Thanks.

ADAM: No, I always liked you guys together.

KENT: Uh, me too.

ADAM: I mean. You don't have to talk about it. I'm just saying I'm sorry.

KENT: Yeah, no, thanks. It's OK. *(Beat.)* I mean, whatever, I had some . . . I wasn't totally . . . *(Beat.)* I'm a professional athlete. It can be hard for us to stick those out. You know?

ADAM: Can be.

*(A moment.)*

KENT: OK! Park this one. Just park it. All the way.

ADAM: *(Simultaneously.)* OK now swing down, make sure you're down on it.

*(A moment. They applaud together.)*

KENT: What did I tell you. What. Did. I. Tell. You.

ADAM: *(Simultaneously.)* If not now when. If not now then tell me when.

*(A moment.)*

KENT: So! Any tips?

ADAM: What?

KENT: About this park. You played here for a while, right?

ADAM: Oh, no, yeah, I was here. After Florida.

KENT: That's right. You hit all the expansion clubs.

ADAM: Uh. Yeah.

KENT: So?

ADAM: You'll do fine. New park. Hitter friendly. Also something about the Colorado altitude. Thin. Air. Something. *(Beat.)* Whatever, who am I talking to? The year you're having. *(Beat.)* I mean, you're on pace, Kent. You're on the pace.

KENT: That's what they tell me. I'm not really thinking about it.

ADAM: Well, you've got, what, thirty-five, now, thirty-six, at the break? So —

KENT: Thirty-seven.

ADAM: Thirty-seven home runs at the break? You've never put up numbers like this. Not this fast.

KENT: If you say so. Like I said I'm not really —

ADAM: Sure. No. Sure. *(Beat.)* But, I mean, come on.

KENT: Hey. One game at a time. One at bat at a time. Anything else, you've gotta just get control of it in your mind, and put a cap on it, otherwise —

ADAM: OK. But. I mean, come on. It's me, Kent. It's Adam.

KENT: So . . . ?

ADAM: So talk to me for real.

KENT: Hey, give me a break, OK? We're only halfway through the season, so don't talk to me like it's definitely gonna happen, because then I'm gonna feel extra stupid when it doesn't. It could easily not.

ADAM: No. I know.

KENT: So OK.

ADAM: That's not what I'm saying.

KENT: Well good. *(Beat.)* Wait, what are you saying?

ADAM: Just. What do you think it is?

KENT: What do I think what is.

ADAM: Come on. This is me.

KENT: Yeah. You said that already.

ADAM: So what do you think is going on?

KENT: OK. Well. First of all. It's happening all over the league.

ADAM: What's happening.

KENT: Uh. The numbers, the huge numbers getting put up.

ADAM: Well, OK, but so then —

KENT: And? It's not like this is some sudden jump for me either. I hit fifty-eight last year.

ADAM: Yes. You were also pretty exceptional last season. Oh, hey, you know who else is having a pretty good year.

KENT: Who.

ADAM: Raul.

KENT: Is he?

ADAM: Up in Toronto.

KENT: That where he is now?

ADAM: Yeah. He's charging back this year. Really on a tear.

KENT: Good for him.

ADAM: Man. I haven't seen that guy in a long time. How's he doing?

KENT: Your guess is as good as mine.

ADAM: Oh. Uh. OK. *(Beat.)* OK! No pitcher. No pitcher. Drill this one. *(A moment. He does an announcer voice and applauds. Alone.)* "He got all of that one . . . long fly ball to deep left field . . . he's gonna run out of room . . . to the wall . . . ! Gone!"
*(A moment.)*

KENT: Is there something you're trying to ask me, Adam?

ADAM: What? What.

KENT: Because if there's something you want to ask me, then I wish that you would go ahead and just fucking ask me instead of roping me into what I thought was going to be like a pleasant conversation about catching up with and old friend that at this point I am no longer enjoying at all.
*(Beat.)*

ADAM: Well, OK, Kent. I mean, I'm not real slow. When we played together, I knew what was going on. I knew. And we were just coming up, and we were young, we were kids, Jesus, I look at these rooks now . . . And also

I can't say what happened after I left. Of course not. All I know are the stats. But what I'd like to think? Is that you stopped. That maybe you felt bad about it, mentally, and that's why you started to struggle. And that maybe you tried to push yourself too hard without them and so that's how you hurt your foot. Maybe that's not what happened, but that is what I'd like to think. But this? Nothing explains this. And so I guess what I'm asking is for you to tell me to my face. 'Cause I'm not a reporter. I'm not Tony. I'm not the fans and I'm not your son. This is just me here. This is just Adam. Asking why you cheated, Kent. Why are you still cheating?

*(A silence. Adam waits. Then can't anymore.)*

ADAM: Um . . .

KENT: *(He points.)* Shh, hey, hold on. Barry's coming up to take his cuts.

ADAM: Oh. Hey.

*(They watch. A silence.)*

KENT: I love that little batting-practice net that the batting-practice pitcher has to stand behind? I love that thing. It's pure fear. It's like. "Please don't hurt me Mr. Awesome Batter. Please don't strike me down with your mighty power." I love that. Look how this guy is throwing. It's like he thinks Barry's gonna kill him. *(Beat.)* You talk to that guy yet today?

ADAM: Who, Barry?

KENT: Oh my God. What a prick, right?

ADAM: Oh. Yeah. I guess.

KENT: What a total prick.

ADAM: Yeah. No. He is. *(Beat.)* Although. I mean. You know.

KENT: What.

ADAM: Just. It's possible that he maybe had to face some things that you and me didn't have to face.

KENT: Like what. What things. *(Beat.)* Oh.

*(A moment. They watch. They react.)*

KENT: Damn.

ADAM: Yeah. That is a sweet swing.

KENT: You're not kidding.

*(A moment.)*

KENT: So OK. Do you remember 1919?

ADAM: What?

KENT: Just —

ADAM: No, Kent, I do not remember 1919, as I was not exactly around.

KENT: Do you remember what happened.

ADAM: I think so. Yeah.

KENT: Black Sox. A handful of gangsters bribes the best team in the game to throw the World Series. So there everybody is. After the biggest thing in American sports just got bought. And the game is dead. Except. The thing back then that almost nobody could do? Was hit one out. Guys were parking fifteen a year, twenty, tops. And that made you a slugger. Not even. Those were flukes. You hit a fly ball and it happens to catch the wind and carry. Nobody's thinking about clearing the wall. It almost never happens. But then who comes along?

ADAM: *(Beat.)* So, OK, you're just not gonna —

KENT: Who comes along, Adam?

ADAM: Babe Ruth.

KENT: Until 1919 he's a pitcher, basically. Most homers he's ever hit in a season is twenty-nine. Second most is eleven. After 1919, he gets traded to the Yankees, and instead of putting him in the rotation, which would be wise since the guy is a great pitcher, they put him in the outfield so he can focus on hitting. In 1920, he hits fifty-four home runs. In 1921? He hits fifty-nine. Nobody had ever done anything close to that. Black Sox broke everybody's heart and people thought it was going to take the game years to recover from that. A decade. If ever. Two seasons later all anybody's talking about is Babe Ruth. Who by the way? Was no angel. And when he hits sixty in 1927 everybody knows that's the best team ever. Fuck the Black Sox. It's Murderer's Row. Gehrig, Combs, Dugan. Ruth.

ADAM: OK, but —

*(Kent puts a hand on Adam's shoulder, silencing him. A moment. Kent looks at Adam earnestly as though he's going to say something else. Then, instead, slides his other hand up Adam's shirt. Adam allows it, not resisting. Kent brings his hand back out after a moment. Clutching a wire and a tiny microphone, a length of duct tape still dangling from it. A moment. Then, Kent brings the microphone deliberately near his mouth and speaks directly into it.)*

KENT: And, yeah, I got shook up a little, with pressure to perform, and I had some injuries, because this game is hard, but I came back from that, and that is one of the things I've done I'm proudest of, and, yeah, you weren't there, because you got traded, because you weren't living up to your potential, because you cracked like a little bitch, even though a guy like you doesn't have half of what I do resting on his shoulders for the survival of the fucking sport, and now you're gonna get in my face with this melodramatic and accusatory horseshit like you can talk from some place of moral superiority when all you really did was fail? Fuck you. Now is there anything else? Because if not, I think we're done.

*(Kent drops the microphone and turns back out. A moment. Kent claps.)*

KENT: OK. That's right. We've got a team here. We have got a team.

*(During this, Adam tears the microphone the rest of the way off and shoves it into his pocket. A long silence. When at last they do speak, it is without looking at each other.)*

ADAM: Well that is a great attitude, Kent.

KENT: What?

ADAM: The Black Sox threw the series because their owners treated them like slaves. We went on strike because our owners had a labor dispute with our union. It's not the same. Babe Ruth? Sure, he, lived on whiskey and cigars and he was really fat and he had a ton of women and he was kind of a cocky bastard, but he played straight, Kent. He played it straight. Man, those guys played the game. Work the count, draw the walk, steal second, take third on the hit and run, score on the sac fly, the actual game —

KENT: This is the game, Adam. I'm playing the game.

ADAM: Yeah everybody's on board. Ownership on down. Why not? The fans are back. So, hey, forget leveling the field, let's all watch rich teams from big cities beat up poor teams from small cities with nothing but home runs. So I don't care if you are the savior of the sport, Kent, because the fact is the sport is fucked. *(Pause.)* So you know what I think? I think it should have been years. A decade. If ever. I think when something like that happens? It's supposed to hurt. Real bad. For a long long time. I think that's how you learn enough so that next time? You approach the thing with a little bit more fucking respect.

*(Pause.)*

KENT: So, what, you got caught?

ADAM: I . . . What? Caught at what.

KENT: I mean they caught you and flipped you, right? You cut a deal?

ADAM: This isn't a movie, Kent. And I never did anything to get caught at.

KENT: OK. So, then, what do you want. A fucking medal?

*(Pause.)*

ADAM: I'm up.

*(Adam starts up the steps.)*

KENT: Rook.

*(A moment. Adam goes. Kent remains, alone. A moment. Then, Kent applauds.)*

KENT: That's it, rook. Keep your head down. *(Pause. Then he applauds again.)* Nice. Don't force it. *(Pause. He applauds.)* There it is. On the screws. *(Pause. Then, to himself.)* On the screws.

# CHECK, PLEASE: TAKE 3
## Jonathan Rand

Comic
Dan, twenties
Girl, twenties

> *A couple are at a restaurant on a first date. He is a movie-trailer an-*
> *nouncer and finds it difficult to talk like a normal person.*

> *(At a restaurant table. Dan speaks in that deep, intense movie-trailer voice.*
> *You know the one.)*

GIRL: Hi there.

DAN: *In a world* where anything can happen . . . one man . . . goes on a date
. . . with a woman . . .
*(Pause.)*

GIRL: It's nice to meet you too.

DAN: Once in a lifetime . . . one moment comes along that changes us . . .
forever . . .

GIRL: *(Lifts up a finger, thinking about speaking.)*

DAN: *She's* from the mean streets of South Central . . .

GIRL: *(Pointing to herself.)* Actually, South *Dakota.*

DAN: *He's* a renegade cop . . .

GIRL: You're a renegade cop?

DAN: . . . Together, they just might make . . . the perfect pair . . .

GIRL: *(Cheerily trying to end the madness.)* OK, let's —

DAN: From Universal Pictures and the producers who brought you *Norbit* . . .

GIRL: OK . . .

DAN: . . . comes the conversation . . . forty-five seconds into the making . . .

GIRL: OK, stop! *(Pause.)* Is there some *reason* you're doing an impression of
that movie-trailer voice?

DAN: That voice . . . is mine . . .

GIRL: *(Not buying it.)* That's really you? That's your job?

DAN: It is . . .
*(Beat.)*

GIRL: OK, that's actually pretty cool . . . Still, it'd be less weird if you just
talked in your normal speaking voice.

DAN: This *is* my normal speaking voice.

GIRL: It is . . . ?

DAN: I've been the official movie-preview voice for so long, I've forgotten how to speak . . . like a normal person . . .

GIRL: Uh-huh.

DAN: My voice makes life . . . harder than you think . . . I've found it difficult . . . to show emotion . . . For example . . . here is what it sounds like when I say . . . something exciting . . . I can't believe my team won the Super Bowl. How about that catch in the game-winning drive. What a play. I'm freaking out. Woo.

GIRL: It does lose something in the translation.

DAN: Or last week . . . when my friend's grandmother died . . . It was hard to sound sincere . . . When I told him *this:* I'm so sorry for your loss . . . Grams was a wonderful woman . . . My condolences to you . . . and your family.

GIRL: It must be hard for you.

DAN: It's made me . . . clinically depressed . . .

GIRL: Well, what if we try to fix your problem?

DAN: I'm fairly certain . . . it can't be fixed . . .

GIRL: We could try . . . Here — give me an example line from one of your movie trailers.

*(He briefly prepares himself, putting his hand over his ear as if he were in a studio.)*

DAN: *In a world* where parakeets rule, one man —

GIRL: OK, there. Say "In a world" again.

DAN: *In a world* . . .

GIRL: Right. But this time, say it like I do. "In a world."

DAN: *In a world* . . .

GIRL: Better. *(It wasn't better.)* Try again.

DAN: *In a world* . . .

GIRL: OK, try saying: "Inside this planet."

DAN: *In a world* . . .

GIRL: All right, forget it. I can't stay if you're gonna talk like that the whole time. *(She gathers her belongings.)*

DAN: Before you go . . . can you do me one favor . . .

GIRL: What?

DAN: Could you give me . . . a ride home . . .

GIRL: You don't have a car?

DAN: I can't . . . afford it . . .

GIRL: You can't afford a car? You're a Hollywood celebrity. Shouldn't you have a lot of money?

*(He puts his hand to his ear as if he's in the studio again.)*

DAN: *In a world* of plastic surgery and million-dollar makeovers . . . *one man* . . . risked it all. *(Beat. In his regular voice.)* And now he's broke and lives with his mom.

# FAT KIDS ON FIRE
Bekah Brunstetter

Seriocomic
Bess, fifteen
Scott, fourteen

> *Florida, July. It's Bess's first day of fat camp, and already the boys be mackin'. (Note: A slash [/] indicates overlapping dialogue.)*

> *(Bess stands center surrounded by her luggage. She is listening to music, on her headphones. She is extremely uncomfortable. It's hot. Scott approaches, he watches her. His soccer shorts sag.)*

SCOTT: Holla.

> *(Bess looks around her. Who the hell is he talking to, even?)*

SCOTT: You have nice legs.

BESS: What?

SCOTT: You have great legs.

BESS: Oh, thanks. *(Pause.)* Really?

SCOTT: Oh come on. I bet niggaz are *always* like, *damn* girl. You've got the best legs here. How tall are you?

BESS: Five eight or something.

SCOTT: Yeah, I like my women tall.

> *(He looks up at her. She looks down at him.)*

BESS: Um — Do you know where I go? With my stuff?

SCOTT: *(Smiling.)* You wanna shack up with this?

BESS: No, I'm just — 'Cause I'm kind of just standing here. The airport shuttle dropped me off. I don't know where to go.

SCOTT: Well, everyone gets assigned to dorms and stuff, that's later, I think. They're just waiting for everyone to get here, so — do you like swimming or what? Pool's over there by the cafeteria. Do you wanna go swimming?

BESS: Right now?

SCOTT: Yeah, come on. I bet you look dope in your suit.

BESS: Are we allowed to like, just go? Whenever we want?

SCOTT: Yeah, come on. We can do whatever.

BESS: Really?

SCOTT: Hell, yeah. Well, pretty much. See, my parents own this shit, I hang out for the summers, I do what I want.

BESS: No rules? Seriously?

SCOTT: OK, here's all you have to know. But if I tell you, you have to kiss me later. I bet you're a *real* good kisser.

BESS: *(Forcing, trying.)* . . . Yeah — I've kissed — *lots* — I mean, all the time — hell, yeah. With frequency, even.

SCOTT: Hell, *Yeah.* OK.

Number one. Don't talk to the really fat ones. It's not good for your rep. One word to them, and they be all UP on your junk, they so *crazy,* they be like we's best friends now, and you be all like NO.

Two — Be real nice to Nurse Joy, your life is in her hands. Don't get on that bitch's bad side or you're shit up a creek if you get swimmer's ear, and bitch don't even care 'cause you were rude to her.

The gazebo's where you go to make out. Stay hydrated. Don't take the green pills at dinner 'cause they make you jumpy. Oh. And make out with me.

BESS: What pills?

SCOTT: Do you have a bikini?

BESS: Yeah.

SCOTT: Awesome. You are not even fat at *all.*

BESS: Yeah — well — comparatively — I mean compared to / other —

SCOTT: Nice hey, do you have any boyfriends at home?

BESS: No, I mean yeah, like a few. Four, five. Seven. But nothing / serious.

SCOTT: What are you doing at fat camp?

BESS: I'm chubby. Like a toddler.

*(Pause. Scott nods.)*

BESS: Yeah, it's 'cause I'm smart, though, that's all, I think, I have other stuff on my mind.

SCOTT: You're so freaking hot.

*(Pause. Bess has no idea what to do, so she begins to ramble with awkward ease.)*

BESS: My mom was an Olympic skier, and my dad did a lot of water polo. They are real into fitness, and I never really have been. Even though they completely forced me to play soccer and swim team and T-ball and gymnastics, and they used to lock me out of the house until I'd ridden my bike around the neighborhood eights times, and it was kind of a big neighborhood, my old house. Once I was walking up that street barefoot, and a snake slid across my bare foot. It was really scary.

*(Scott just looks at her.)*

BESS: Also, I like to draw.

SCOTT: What's your name again?

BESS: Bess.

SCOTT: Awesome, so do you like me, or what?

BESS: You — you're — you're um —

SCOTT: I'm Scott.

(*Extends his hand, takes hers, kisses it with ridiculous bravado.*)

SCOTT: I pick you.

BESS: Pick me for what?

SCOTT: My summer girlfriend.

BESS: (*Embarrassed.*) OK.

SCOTT: You are so hot.

(*Bess has no idea what to do.*)

BESS: It's hot out here. Is it always this hot?

SCOTT: This is *nothing*. Wait a few weeks and they start fainting in the soccer field. Kids dropping like flies. Hey, you'll get a good tan, though.

BESS: People faint?

SCOTT: Yeah well usually just the really fat ones. They fry like eggs. Like fat-kid omelettes.

BESS: I'm Bess, by the way. Did I say that? It's short for Besseda. That's also the name of a few hotels in Bulgaria, so.

SCOTT: And I'm your boyfriend. So go put your bathing suit on, shawty! You can go into the bathroom in the cafeteria. It's in to the right.

BESS: OK.

SCOTT: Can I watch?

BESS: What? No.

SCOTT: Come on. I'm your boyfriend.

BESS: Nah, you don't want to see all that.

SCOTT: Hell, yeah. Let's go swimming. Meet you at the pool, honey.

(*He saunters off.*)

BESS: B — bye! (*She watches him go.*) B — boyfriend? OK. Boyfriend. Right. (*She smiles at herself.*) Boyfriend.

# GOOD BOYS AND TRUE
Roberto Aguirre-Sacasa

Dramatic
Brandon, teens
Justin, teens

> *Brandon and Justin are students at an exclusive Catholic prep school.*
> *They are buddies. Brandon is a BMOC. Justin is a more introverted*
> *type. The football team recently watched a video of a boy forcing a girl*
> *to have sex with him, and the tape has been found by the school ad-*
> *ministration. The boy on the tape looks like Brandon, but he denies it's*
> *him. Here, Justin confronts him about it.*

JUSTIN: Uh, hi, Brandon.

BRANDON: Oh, hey, Justin.

JUSTIN: What happened last night? I thought you were gonna call me.

BRANDON: Yeah, I was; sorry about that.

JUSTIN: I was actually *waiting* for your call, Brandon. (During which time, I finished this week's *and* next week's Cicero translations, which — before you even ask — yes, you can borrow.)

BRANDON: Sweet —

JUSTIN: I'd give you my AP bio homework —

BRANDON: Dr. Justin Simmons, soon to be —

JUSTIN: But oh, that's right, we're not lab partners anymore. On top of which, I'm *pissed* at you!

BRANDON: My mom and I were talking —

JUSTIN: All night long?

BRANDON: Yeah, because — *(Minibeat.)* — Look, don't freak out, but I told her, OK? About Dartmouth.

JUSTIN: You did?

BRANDON: Yeah, so — we had to, like, discuss it and stuff. Call my grand-parents . . .

JUSTIN: Waitwaitwait: Weren't we gonna wait until *I* heard from Dartmouth and then tell our parents together?

BRANDON: Were we?

JUSTIN: It was kind of a *pact*, Brandon. We kind of *vowed.*

BRANDON: I told my mom about Dartmouth, Justin, to defuse the situation created by her asking me about the videotape.

*(Short pause, then.)*

JUSTIN: *WHAT?*

BRANDON: Coach *Shea* gave it to her.

JUSTIN: *(Freaking out.)* Fuck! How did Shea — ?

BRANDON: He found it because some freshmen assholes left it in the VCR upstairs.

JUSTIN: Fuck! But I thought Mitchell had the tape.

BRANDON: Yeah, but this is *Mitchell.* Probably he made copies and, and started *selling* them.

JUSTIN: (Fucking idiot . . . )

BRANDON: Shea thought it was me, so he went to my mom because he and my dad are friends.

JUSTIN: But it *isn't* you on the tape —

BRANDON: Obviously —

JUSTIN: OK, well, that's a relief, since it's not like we've talked about it, Brandon, and some people are saying it looks like you. Plus, no one's taken credit for it, which — if you examine the list of likely suspects (i.e., your troglodyte teammates) — is pretty uncharacteristic.

BRANDON: It looks like me, whatever, but it also looks like Miller, it also looks like Daniel, it also looks like — well, I mean, it sort of looks like you, too, stud.

JUSTIN: *(Big-time sarcastic.)* Oh, yeah, it was me, sorry, I forgot.

BRANDON: I'm just playing devil's advocate. *(Beat.)* Anyway, you were there with us, you *saw* the tape —

JUSTIN: I *left,* Brandon, as soon as I realized —

BRANDON: What do you want, a *medal? (Beat. Softer.)* You're not on the team with us, you had a choice.

JUSTIN: You're captain, you can do whatever you want.

BRANDON: Yeah, but I was, like . . . *transfixed,* OK? And . . . and it *did* feel wrong, watching the tape. But also . . . not *that* wrong. It was kind of . . .

JUSTIN: Stimulating?

BRANDON: Kind of.

JUSTIN: What, you, like . . . got a woodie?

BRANDON: *(Are you kidding?)* A *what?* A *woodie?*

JUSTIN: Or whatever.

BRANDON: An *erection,* you mean?

JUSTIN: Yes.

BRANDON: I am *not* discussing my erections with you in public, Justin.

JUSTIN: Anyway, well, it can't be Trevor on the tape, he's got red hair; it can't be Ridgeway, he's not big enough

BRANDON: Maybe it's Mitchell? (And that's why he "found" it in his locker?)

JUSTIN: Possibly. *(Beat, he thinks about it.)* But why would Mitchell — ?

BRANDON: *I don't know. (Beat.)* Because he has no sense of, of *propriety*.

JUSTIN: If you know, and you're *not* telling me —

BRANDON: Look, it's stupid — it's lame — and ironically, it's probably not even someone who goes here. *(Beat.)* And my mom gave Coach Shea the tape back this morning, so it's not like it's an issue anymore, and — and we shouldn't *obsess* over it, and you shouldn't turn this into one of your — you know, *things*.

JUSTIN: Things?

BRANDON: Things you fixate on, Rain Man.

JUSTIN: — OK.

BRANDON: And I'm sorry. That I didn't call you last night. I meant to.

JUSTIN: I just . . . I fucking *hate* this place sometimes, you know? All the fucking columns, all the goddamn marble, it's *suffocating*.

BRANDON: *(Duh.)* It's *high school*, Justin. The Roman Empire fell over fifteen hundred years ago, and we're *still* taking Latin.

JUSTIN: Hey, can we *please* not be on opposite teams today?

BRANDON: Uhm — we always are.

JUSTIN: Yeah, OK, fine, but just *once* can't we be teammates?

BRANDON: Nope, and how many times do I have to explain why? *(Beat.)* When we're on the same team — when we're both *sweating* and in close proximity to each other — I can*not* keep my hands off your hard, *hard* body, and that makes everyone around us *incredibly* uncomfortable. *(Short pause as Justin looks at Brandon.)*

JUSTIN: Sick. You're a sick, *sick* bastard —

# HEADS

E. M. Lewis

Dramatic
Michael Aprés, thirty-four
Jack Velazquez, twenty-nine

> *While covering the war in Iraq, journalist Michael Aprés and photo-journalist Jack Velazquez are taken hostage. Their captors accuse Michael of working with the CIA and threaten to kill him, which spurs the two men into a bloodily unsuccessful escape attempt. In the aftermath, Jack decides to tell their captors that he's the one who has been working for the CIA. Michael can't accept that it might just be true.*

> *(Aprés sits near the wall, with his arms wrapped tightly around his knees. Velazquez still lies in the same place he was before, in the middle of the cell. His head is resting on the scraps of Aprés's T-shirt.)*

VELAZQUEZ: So . . . How about that moss? *(Long pause.)* You gotta talk to me sometime.

APRÉS: I'm thinking.

VELAZQUEZ: Think out loud.

APRÉS: *(Beat.)* This is either the best thing anyone has ever done for me or the worst thing anyone has done to me. And . . . I can't figure out which. *(Beat.)* You're lying.

VELAZQUEZ: No.

APRÉS: *(Pause.)* You're a journalist. We're journalists.

VELAZQUEZ: Yeah.

APRÉS: And you also, in your spare time, work for the CIA.

VELAZQUEZ: Yeah.

APRÉS: What do you do for them?

VELAZQUEZ: What I do.

APRÉS: What?

VELAZQUEZ: I did what I do. I sold them some pictures.

APRÉS: Some pictures.

VELAZQUEZ: Some pictures. Of some people.

APRÉS: What people?

VELAZQUEZ: If I told you, then I'd have to kill you.

APRÉS: That's not funny. Why would you . . . *(Beat.)* You're lying to me.

VELAZQUEZ: No.

APRÉS: I don't believe you sold pictures to the CIA. Why would you do that?

VELAZQUEZ: Money, stupid.

APRÉS: No.

VELAZQUEZ: What do you think I live on? How do you think I live?

APRÉS: Not that way. You're a journalist.

VELAZQUEZ: I sell pictures. I am a guy who takes pictures and sells pictures. That's what I do. Do you have any idea what the real world is like? I have a fixer who can speak Arabic, Kurdish, and English and can drive like Dale Earnhardt. He's poor enough and crazy enough to take me anywhere. We drive around. We listen to the radios. I have seven. When something happens, we try to get there first, and we never do, but I shove my way up to the front and shoot as fast as I can. Jalal holds the Canon while I shoot with the Nikon. When I get something, we bail, and try to upload it to the wire from the car before the other seventy guys there get their pictures on the wire, because if you aren't best, you gotta be first or you don't get shit.

APRÉS: There was nothing in all that about the CIA. Or did I miss it?

VELAZQUEZ: I sell pictures. Sometimes . . . if you know the right people and go the right places, the CIA buys pictures.

APRÉS: You go places, people allow you in places, because you're a journalist. And then you take advantage of that by —

VELAZQUEZ: What side are you on?

APRÉS: *(Beat.)* I'm a journalist.

VELAZQUEZ: What side are you on?

APRÉS: I am not political.

VELAZQUEZ: Bullshit!

APRÉS: A journalist who serves one side or the other cannot serve the truth. We are required to remain free of associations and activities that could compromise —

VELAZQUEZ: You sound like a fucking book.

APRÉS: — compromise our integrity or damage our credibility.

VELAZQUEZ: Lift up your shirt and look at yourself, and tell me you're not political. *(Beat.)* They are terrorists.

APRÉS: *(About Velazquez.)* I thought we were on the same side. *(Beat.)* You're the reason they took us. Aren't you?

VELAZQUEZ: *(Beat.)* Maybe.

APRÉS: We don't even look alike. I don't understand why they . . . why they thought . . . *(Beat.)* Why didn't you tell me?

VELAZQUEZ: We were getting along so well. *(Beat.)* I thought I could get us out.

APRÉS: When they took me . . . *(Pause, then more firmly.)* When they took me before, and . . . they asked me if I was CIA. If I was working for the CIA. I told you that. And you didn't say anything.

VELAZQUEZ: *(Beat.)* I really, really, really don't want to die.

*(Silence.)*

APRÉS: Then why tell them now? *(Silence.)* Why tell them now?

VELAZQUEZ: Because. *(Pause.)* I sold pictures of Iraqi terrorists —

APRÉS: *(Overlapping.)* For money.

VELAZQUEZ: *(Overlapping.)* — pictures of Iraqi terrorists to the CIA. And I was right to —

APRÉS: You were wrong! How can we report the truth objectively if we are part of the story?

VELAZQUEZ: There is no objectivity! Every fucking network is embedded up the American military's ass, and you talk about —

APRÉS: I'm against that. I'm against it. I'm against this whole preemptive quagmire, but that's my personal belief system, Jack! In my role as a journalist —

VELAZQUEZ: Your role as a journalist.

APRÉS: What you did puts all journalists in danger! If they see us as partisan, if they see us —

VELAZQUEZ: You want they should bomb another grade school? Another mosque? Another grocery store like the one in Baquba? With little veiled Sunni grandmothers and radishes blown all to fuck? Another unit of American soldiers to go home without any arms? I sold pictures of terrorists to the CIA, and it wasn't wrong. But . . . *(Beat.)* I did it. And you didn't.

APRÉS: *(Pause.)* They'll kill you if you tell them.

VELAZQUEZ: They'll kill you if I don't. And what kind of fucked-up choice is that?

*(A moment. Aprés pushes the heels of his hands into his eyes. His fists are clenched.)*

APRÉS: But they'll . . . they'll still kill me, Jack. Won't they?

VELAZQUEZ: No.

APRÉS: You don't know that. You don't . . . They'll kill us both. I . . . *(Beat.)* This is not a good plan.

VELAZQUEZ: *(With emphasis.)* It's all I got. *(Silence.)* Move where I can see you.

APRÉS: No. *(Pause, looking at Velazquez.)* Do you think they'll believe you? When you tell them you did it?

*(After a moment, Velazquez nods. Aprés takes a breath. Then another.)*

APRÉS: I can't breathe. *(Pause, begins to hyperventilate.)* You shouldn't . . . but . . . you shouldn't have, but . . . I can't . . .

VELAZQUEZ: I'm doing it.

APRÉS: I'm having trouble . . . breathing. I never . . .

VELAZQUEZ: If you're going to hyperventilate and pass out, do it over here where I can see you.

*(Aprés gets awkwardly to his feet. He puts his hand on his chest. He moves into Velazquez's sight line and sits awkwardly, a few feet from him. Taking in air desperately.)*

VELAZQUEZ: I want to memorize right now.

APRÉS: Right now is . . . fucked.

VELAZQUEZ: *(Smiles a little.)* Put your head between your knees.

*(Aprés hangs his head down between his knees. Velazquez watches him.)*

VELAZQUEZ: I'd hate to be a blind person.

APRÉS: I . . . don't know why . . . I can't —

VELAZQUEZ: Quit talking, dummy.

*(Aprés breathes. After a few moments, his breath begins to slow, but he keeps his head down. Velazquez lifts his hands up and makes a frame with them, capturing Aprés.)*

# MARGO VEIL
## Len Jenkin

Comic
Hy Hepstein, fifties
Margo, twenties

> *Hy Hepstein is an old-time Broadway talent agent. Margo is a would-be*
> *actress. She's about to give up on New York, and he offers her a strange job.*

*(Hy Hepstein's shabby office. Broadway show posters, a desk.)*

HEPSTEIN: Honey, this is a talent agency, not the loan department. You're
down on your luck, but something'll turn up.

MARGO: No, Hy, this life isn't for me. My parents were right.

HEPSTEIN: Parents? I thought girls like you, they grew them in a vat in
Minnesota.

MARGO: They said go to New York, Margo, give it a try, get it out of your system. *(Beat.)* Well, I tried.

HEPSTEIN: I guess you have. You know, I went to see *A Distant Candelabra*. It
stunk. You stunk in it. Who wrote that thing?

MARGO: Arthur Vine's his name.

HEPSTEIN: Handsome?

MARGO: Some of the girls thought so . . .

HEPSTEIN: Artistic? Deep?

MARGO: Some of the girls were really into his depth . . .

HEPSTEIN: You sleep with him?

MARGO: I . . . I . . .

HEPSTEIN: Forget it, honey. We're all young and stupid once.
*(An uncomfortable silence.)*

MARGO: What's that odd statue on your desk, Hy? I never noticed it before.

HEPSTEIN: Just a piece of tourist junk my wife bought years ago. Near the
Baltic Sea. Decorating your office, she said.

MARGO: Looks like an owl.

HEPSTEIN: Yeah. Maybe it does. *(Beat.)* Look, sweetheart, if you're serious
about going home, I got a way you can get there, and pick up a
few bucks besides. Come to think of it, you'll even get a new dress out
of the deal.

MARGO: Fairy godmother, Hy! Keep talking.

HEPSTEIN: An unusual setup. Nobody in the family wants to take the time, or maybe they're not interested. Hearts of stone.

MARGO: Come on, what's the job?

HEPSTEIN: It's an — acting job. You play the role of the grieving relative.

MARGO: What?

HEPSTEIN: Look, honey, you wanna get home? There's really nothing to this. You get train fare and five hundred dollars. Seems the railroad doesn't allow dead bodies to travel unaccompanied. You ride with the coffin to a town called, uh, Rapid City.

MARGO: Rapid City! That's only a hundred miles from Colby, my hometown.

HEPSTEIN: What a coincidence. You take the train from Grand Central, they put the coffin in the baggage car at Scranton, you sign for it, escort it to Rapid City. You want the job?

MARGO: Of course I do.

*(Hepstein hands her a ticket.)*

HEPSTEIN: Here's your train ticket. You'll get the money in Rapid City at the Feldman Mortuary. The anonymous party paying for all this will leave an envelope for you with the mortuary manager.

MARGO: Five hundred dollars?

HEPSTEIN: Yep.

MARGO: Hy, I love you.

HEPSTEIN: I love you too. When you get home, don't forget to mail me my ten percent.

MARGO: What about the new dress?

HEPSTEIN: Already paid for. You get to pick it out at some store on Fifth — Valentino.

MARGO: Valentino. Well, get me. At least I'm going home in style.

HEPSTEIN: Don't get too stylish, sweetheart. You better make that dress — black.

*(Margo steps behind a folding screen, changing clothes. Old outfit flies over the screen.)*

HEPSTEIN: *(On phone.)* Louise, get me Sally Struthers, and a chicken salad on rye, heavy on the mayo . . .

# ON AN AVERAGE DAY
John Kolvenbach

Dramatic
Jack, thirties
Bobby, twenties

*Bobby is a more than slightly crazy fellow who lives physically in the home of his dead parents, but who really lives pretty much in his own mind. His father abandoned him and his brother Jack when they were kids. Then Jack took off. But he has come back, after being gone for many years. Here, they are getting reacquainted.*

ROBERT: You wanna know something?

JACK: What's that.

ROBERT: *(Positively.)* And I don't even know if I'm gonna be able to get enough emphasis on the thing to actually convey the whole size of it, but us in the kitchen at the same time together? Here's me and apparently there you are? I can't even start to say how *strange* that is.

JACK: Well, cheers,Bob.

ROBERT: 'Cause I already told you about the metal thing and the "who's gonna scratch me around every corner" thing. Knowing these things are outside the Norm, makes me question like: Are you actually even *standing* there.

JACK: I'm right here.

ROBERT: Which is borderline Miraculous, Jack, the thing is *Religious* either way, is what I'm trying to make *Clear*, is that either I'm somebody who's having *Visions*, or it's the other thing, which is: Here you Are.

JACK: Yeah. *(Beat.)* Well, it's been a while, I guess.
*(Pause.)*

ROBERT: Listen, I know what you're gonna say.

JACK: Bobby, stop it, all right?

ROBERT: I'm Curious.

JACK: Will you Stop?

ROBERT: But it's my whole *mind*, Jack, I can't open my mouth, or it automatically comes *out*.

JACK: So stop talking, how about.

ROBERT: No, but is this one of those things where you're gonna be around for like a *month*?

JACK: Bob.

ROBERT: Is that a possibility?

JACK: I said this.

ROBERT: Is a month, like, in the *vicinity*?

JACK: No. It's not in the vicinity.

ROBERT: *(Encouraged by Jack's specificity.)* So this is what I'm asking. Is it a *six*-month kind of thing?

JACK: I'm here now.

ROBERT: So it's like a day-to-day thing, it's like a who-knows thing.

JACK: I'm not Staying.

ROBERT: But at least through the trial, though, right? To the end at least.

JACK: The trial.

ROBERT: Which, the length is sort of up in the air, so you'd be in one of those day-to-day deals.

JACK: The Trial.

ROBERT: (It's not all Grim and Drag, Jack.)

JACK: (What?)

ROBERT: (There's some Upside in there.)

JACK: (What are we talking about.)

ROBERT: (You know how if you get put in contact with individuals you might not *know*, normally, how there's some Information there?)

JACK: (OK.)

ROBERT: (This is one of those.)

JACK: (What is.)

ROBERT: (Only I gotta say, the only information I have so far is: Who the Fuck *Are* these people?)

JACK: (Who?]

ROBERT: *(An outburst.)* The *One* Guy, God, the FAT SCHMUCK.

JACK: Whoa, Bobby.

ROBERT: You should *See* this guy!

JACK: From the trial?

ROBERT: My *motive*, like he's got access to my *mind* all of a sudden.

JACK: A lawyer.

ROBERT: A *Douche* bag.

JACK: A Lawyer, this is.

ROBERT: What's the *Matter* with that guy?

JACK: I don't know —

ROBERT: The People *Versus*, like suddenly he's a *plural*, he's the royal *We*, (fucking queen.)

JACK: A prosecutor.

ROBERT: ('Member that time in scouts Jack? And Jimmy Rapanti borrowed my hatchet or something and then he kept saying it was his and so you and me went over to his house and kicked his ass?)

JACK: *(Warily.)* . . . Why.

ROBERT: Remember that?

JACK: Maybe.

ROBERT: I think about that sometimes.

JACK: In what context.

ROBERT: In like, what if the Fat Schmuck is in the phone book?

JACK: The lawyer?

ROBERT: What if the fat load is *listed?*

JACK: Bob.

ROBERT: How about in the context of you and me pulling into his driveway with the lights off, How about you and me in *that* context?

JACK: *(Quite firmly.)* Bob? That is a Very Bad idea.

ROBERT: Remember that Jimmy Rapanti thing?

JACK: It's a Bad idea, Bobby.

ROBERT: That whole year, You remember that? People were half afraid to even *talk* to me that year.

JACK: That's a *positive?*

ROBERT: Who talks to the Lone Ranger?

JACK: What?

ROBERT: *Nobody.*

JACK: What about Tonto?

ROBERT: That's what I'm saying, so maybe you and I weren't exactly *popular.*

JACK: You were *seven.*

ROBERT: I was *Right*, was what I was.

JACK: You were *what?*

ROBERT: Jimmy's *face*, and I don't wanna sound like I *enjoyed* something —

JACK: You were *Right?*

ROBERT: Jimmy Understood that we came from a thing of *Fury* —

JACK: *(Suddenly, fiercely.)* IT WASN'T YOUR HATCHET.
(*Pause.*)

ROBERT: It didn't turn *out* to be my hatchet.

JACK: What does that even *mean?*

ROBERT: We *thought* it was, Jack.

JACK: *So?*

ROBERT: So at the *time*, I'm saying, that was a Justified thing at that *time*, given our thinking at that particular —

JACK: Bob. We Are Not Going to Anybody's House. We are Not Pulling into Anybody's *Driveway* with the Lights off, All *right? (Pause.)* Bob.

ROBERT: All *right*.

JACK: I'm Serious.

ROBERT: I'm not saying let's go get in the *car*, Jack, Jesus, I'm just thinking about how here you are and suddenly that's a *Possibility*.

JACK: It's *Not* a possibility.

ROBERT: O*K*.

JACK: And even if it *Was*, Bob, if it was an *Option*, it would be a *Stupid* option, OK? And *not* Justified and not anything there's even a *Chance* of us doing.

ROBERT: Jesus, I'm *talking*. Guy can *talk*. Options happen to be *Optional*, Jack, that's most of their whole *makeup*. We may not necessarily *choose* to, but isn't Great to know we *can* —

JACK: IT WASN'T YOUR *HATCHET*.

*(Pause.)*

ROBERT: *(Cowed.)* Christ Jack, all *right*, I was a little *kid*, it's not even what I'm *talking* about.

JACK: *(Exasperated, massaging his upper nose.)* (Jesus Christ.)

ROBERT: I'm saying good to see you, is my whole point: good to see you around the kitchen again, is all I'm saying.

JACK: Oh, *that's* what you're saying.

ROBERT: Yeah and How're you doing, that kind of thing.

JACK: (I forgot what you were like.)

ROBERT: You have a headache?

JACK: *(Not asking.)* (How long have I been here.)

ROBERT: *(Offering the bourbon.)* You wanna give this guy a little action?

JACK: *(Asking.)* How long have I Been here?

ROBERT: Take a smidgen outta this dog here, Jack, good for you.

*(Jack accepts the bottle. He drinks.)*

JACK: *(Re: something unknown.)* (. . . goddammit.)

*(Pause.)*

ROBERT: *(A kind of peace offering.)* You wanna hop in the shower, get off some of that road grime or anything . . . thing's working again, like I told you . . .

*(Pause.)*

ROBERT: *(Another attempt to begin a peaceful exchange.)* Out of the blue, thing gets very enthusiastic all of a sudden.

JACK: *(Softening, engaging.)* You two have that in common.

ROBERT: The shower and me.

JACK: Very enthusiastic all of sudden.

ROBERT: Me and the shower.

JACK: Yeah.

ROBERT: You might wanna add your*self* to that list you got there, Jack.

JACK: *(With a little laugh.)* . . . I'll do that.

ROBERT: Know what I'm saying?

JACK: *(Opening his second beer.)* Guess it must run in the family.

ROBERT: *(Re: Jack's beer.)* (See? now you got two out, you don't have to get another one out this time.)

JACK: (It's a great system, Bob.)

*(A pause.)*

ROBERT: *(Making conversation.)* I'm telling you, Jack, out of *no*where, this thing. Thing starts acting like a Shower again.

JACK: Fascinating.

ROBERT: It actually messed up some stuff I had stored in the tub in there, got a whole bunch of belongings I had all Soaked and pretty much ruined.

JACK: You had some stuff in the shower?

ROBERT: Some newspapers got all ruined.

JACK: You had newspapers in the *shower?*

ROBERT: I had a collection.

JACK: Of *newspapers?*

ROBERT: Anytime there was an anonymous body found somewhere, somebody they couldn't figure out who it was, I would save the paper.

JACK: *(Beat.) Why?*

ROBERT: So if, you know, if a whole bunch of people were burned beyond recognition, anything with an unidentified dead person, I would save that day's edition, just in case.

JACK: In case *What?*

ROBERT: I expanded it to like, crank callers and any kind of kidnapper type, anybody Unidentified, I would save all of those papers, and obviously that's almost everyday's thing, took up a lot of room. So why not stick 'em in the shower eventually (thing hasn't worked in a decade), and it got to be a big pile.

JACK: Just in case *What*, Bobby?
   *(Pause.)*
JACK: Bob?
ROBERT: *(Beat. A confession.)* . . . In case one of the unidentified people turns
   out to be someone I know.
JACK: Like who.
ROBERT: . . . Or in case one turns out to be Me.

# PERFECT HARMONY
## Andrew Grosso and The Essentials

Seriocomic
Philip, eighteen
Tobi, at least forty

> *Philip Fellowes V is a senior and soloist in The Acafellas, a high-school,*
> *a cappella powerhouse and seventeen-time national champions. Philip's*
> *father, Philip Fellowes IV, was also an Acafella, and Philip's grandfather,*
> *the first Philip Fellowes IV, founded The Acafellas (although it was orig-*
> *inally known as The Acafellows back then). Tobi McClintoch is a world-*
> *famous "voice whisperer." Philip is tormented by a desire to win nationals*
> *and continue the Fellowes tradition of a cappella excellence. In his quest*
> *to further the Fellowes's legacy, he has kicked his best friend out of the*
> *group, taken over as pitch, and is now struggling in vain to sing his tenor*
> *one solos. As a last resort, he has come to Tobi to see if she can help.*

TOBI MCCLINTOCH: *(To the audience.)* When he opened his mouth at our first appointment, I could hear the fear of failing, the rejection of his father, the feeling of abandonment by his friend. I'm a voice whisperer. We have outside voices we share with the world; I hear the inside voice, the pain inside us and desires. I think of my students like an onion, and I have to peel back the layers.
*(Enter Philip.)*
PHILIP: Hello.
TOBI: God, your pain. It's so deep.
PHILIP: I heard you can help me.
TOBI: I hear you can help you.
PHILIP: I'm sorry, I don't understand.
TOBI: I'm sorry you don't understand.
PHILIP: What?
TOBI: God, your pain is a like a chasm of despair.
PHILIP: I was told that if I came to you, you could help me.
TOBI: You should have been told that if you came to me, you could help you.
PHILIP: I need help, I can't sing high enough.
TOBI: You need help, you can't sing inside enough.

PHILIP: Why are you talking like this?

TOBI: Why are you talking like this? Philip, we all —

PHILIP: How did you know my name?

TOBI: You said it the moment you opened your mouth. Your every word drips with it. You came into my office and your outer voice said "Hello" but I heard your inner voice say, "Excuse me, are you Tobi McClintoch the world-famous vocal therapist? My name is Philip Fellowes the Fifth or Fourth or maybe Sixth. God, I don't even know who I am. My grandfather, my father, and now my best friend have all abandoned me, my connections are all severed. And I'm locked in a mutually destructive relationship with the former pitch of, and my best friend in, our a cappella group, the national champions, The Acafellas."

PHILIP: Acafellowes.

TOBI: That's not what it said.

PHILIP: I don't need friends or connections. I just need help with my voice.

TOBI: *(Correcting him.)* Voices, Philip, voices! We all have our outside voices we share with the world; but I can help you hear the inner voice, your pains, your desires. I work like an onion. We all have our perfect voice inside us, and the more complicated our problems, the greater our emotional and physical duress, the greater the layers we have to peel through to find it. If you want to work with me, you'll have to be willing to peel back the layers.

PHILIP: Will it help me sing first tenor?

TOBI: It'll help you sing Fifth Philip.

PHILIP: Can Fifth Philip sing first tenor?

TOBI: Can Fifth Philip fill first tenor?

PHILIP: How long will it take?

TOBI: A few months of sessions twice a week.

PHILIP: I only have one week.

TOBI: You only have one voice.

PHILIP: I only have one week.

TOBI: Nothing works that fast.

PHILIP: I need something.

TOBI: You can't cure anything in a week. Only two things work instantly in this world: love and drugs.

*(Philip spins and sprints to the exit. Tobi turns to the audience.)*

# SATURN RETURNS
## Noah Haidle

Dramatic
28 (Gustin Novak), twenty-eight
Loretta, twenty-eight

> *Gustin Novak, the central character in* Saturn Returns, *is portrayed at three stages of his life. When we first meet him he is eighty-eight years old. We then see him at fifty-eight and, finally, at age twenty-eight. Gustin's wife Loretta died young, but here she is very much alive. 28 (Gustin) and Loretta have come home from a concert and are having a fight.*

28: Baby.

LORETTA: Do not baby me.

28: Your arms do not look fat in that dress.

LORETTA: But they look heavy.

28: Heavy, yes.

LORETTA: Heavy but not fat.

28: There's a difference.

LORETTA: And what is that?

28: One is heavy and one is fat.

    Two very different words.

LORETTA: I don't see the difference.

28: Come downstairs.

LORETTA: I'm going to bed.

    (*She goes to the bedroom.*)

28: Please.

    Baby.

    Baby!

    Just talk to me.

    (*She comes out in her slip.*)

28: Baby.

    Come on.

    Just talk to me.

    (*She marches down the stairs and sits in the chair with a humph.*)

LORETTA: You wanna talk, let's talk.

Huh?

I don't hear any words coming out of your mouth.

28: Baby

LORETTA: No, really. What is it that you wanted to say?

28: It wasn't a particular conversation I had in mind, I just —

LORETTA: — This is the most uncomfortable chair I have ever sat in.

28: Now you see why I prefer the floor.

LORETTA: How hard is it to make a chair?

28: I don't know.

LORETTA: I'm freezing.

28: Here's my jacket.

LORETTA: Thank you.

28: You're welcome.

LORETTA: I'm still mad.

28: I'm letting you be mad.

This is me letting you be mad at me.

LORETTA: You're not letting me be mad if you're talking about it.

28: So I can't talk about letting you be mad.

LORETTA: No.

You cannot.

28: I'll talk about something else.

LORETTA: Good.

28: I'll talk about how beautiful you looked tonight.

LORETTA: Looked? Looked?

Past tense.

28: Look.

Look.

But there.

At the symphony.

When I held your hand.

Like this.

*(He holds her hand.)*

LORETTA: You don't get to hold my hand.

*(She pushes his hand away.)*

28: But I have to demonstrate.

LORETTA: Fine.

You're holding my hand only for the purpose of demonstrating a point.

*(He holds her hand.)*

28: That's the only purpose.

To demonstrate.

And I was holding your hand.

And the music played.

And I looked over.

Like this I looked.

And I saw you.

In the dark.

But your eyes were still bright.

LORETTA: How bright?

28: More bright than words can carry.

LORETTA: That bright?

28: That bright.

And we were holding hands.

And.

I'd never been happier in my life.

*(The symphony rises.)*

LORETTA: Never?

28: Not once.

LORETTA: Not once.

28: And I knew.

I have known.

That this is the person I will grow old with.

Grow tired with.

Who's eyes I will watch get wrinkled.

Who will be the mother of my children.

And someone will have her eyes.

And I will see her eyes in another.

LORETTA: You're going to make me cry.

28: And I thought I hope I die first.

Because I cannot imagine the world without you in it.

LORETTA: You thought all that just when we were sitting there.

28: I thought all that.

LORETTA: OK.

I'm not mad at you anymore.

28: Good. I hate it when you're mad at me.

LORETTA: I belong to you.

28: No, we belong to each other.

LORETTA: You can kiss me if you would like.

28: If I would like. If?

LORETTA: What kind of kiss should it be?

28: One without a name.

LORETTA: I'm ready.

28: Let's meet halfway.

LORETTA: OK. We'll meet halfway.

> *(They meet halfway and kiss. They kiss deeply. And it begins to snow outside. The kissing gets hotter. And they're on the floor.)*

LORETTA: Not here.

28: Why not?

LORETTA: I like our bed.

28: Our bed.

LORETTA: Ours.

> *(She looks out the window.)*

LORETTA: Look.

It's beginning to snow.

28: So it is.

LORETTA: It's winter.

28: It is.

Now it is winter.

LORETTA: It comes every year.

28: It has to.

LORETTA: And now it's beginning.

28: Yes.

Now it is beginning.

> *(She kisses him and runs up the stairs laughing.)*

LORETTA: *(Offstage.)* What are you waiting for?

28: Nothing.

LORETTA: *(Offstage.)* I'm taking my clothes off!

28: No.

I'm not waiting for anything.

# STRETCH
## Susan Bernfield

Dramatic
Orderly, about nineteen
Orderly's Bud, the same age

> *Every day after work, the Orderly and his Bud hang out in the Bud's basement, smoke pot, and watch TV. They've grown up in a small town in Ohio, without much hope or guidance for the future. The Bud works at the mall, and the Orderly has a job in a nursing home. The Orderly is finding he likes the work; he likes feeling that he can be of use, and he's begun to connect the stories he hears from the old people in the home with the lack of a narrative or purpose in his own life. His Bud stands still, is interested only in the next possible high. Meanwhile, the Orderly is slowly discovering that he may want to make something of himself.*

*(In the basement. The Orderly and his Bud, watching TV, stoned.)*

ORDERLY'S BUD: So whatcha wanna do?

ORDERLY: I dunno.

*(Beat.)*

ORDERLY'S BUD: We could go see my sister.

ORDERLY: The methhead or the one with twelve kids?

ORDERLY'S BUD: Which one you think?

ORDERLY: I honestly got no idea, man.

ORDERLY'S BUD: She's not such a methhead.

ORDERLY: How can you be not *such* a methhead, dude —

ORDERLY'S BUD: Well. Well, what're you on, man? You're stoned.

ORDERLY: Yeah, but —

ORDERLY'S BUD: Pot dealer's on the edge, right? Not gonna be easy t'get this shit.

ORDERLY: No?

ORDERLY'S BUD: Profit margin sucks. Maybe it's time to move it on up.

ORDERLY: You're shittin' me. C'mon, man, I thought you liked your teeth.

*(Orderly's Bud kinda chuckles.)*

ORDERLY: And your brain. That shit makes you dumb.

ORDERLY'S BUD: Whadda I got to lose!

*(They kinda keep chuckling.)*

ORDERLY: Your teeth.

*(They do a person-with-no-teeth imitation, cracking each other up in the process.)*

ORDERLY'S BUD: *(With his gums.)* Hey man, let's go down to the mall and get us some smoothies!

*(Back to normal, laughing.)*

ORDERLY: Dude, these guys don't go to the mall, they're too busy suckin' potato chips till they liquify and go down whatever's left of their throats.

ORDERLY'S BUD: Oh, man, is that it? 'Cause nobody's ever out at the mall anymore, man, I'm always like —

ORDERLY: They're all out blowing up their fucking houses.

ORDERLY'S BUD: Cookin' it up and blowin' up their houses. Blam! Pow!

*(He continues to giggle.)*

ORDERLY: If I'm gonna blow some shit up, man, I'm just gonna go down sign up for the army, y'know, go to fuckin' Iraq. Man. What's the point o' gettin' blown up here?

ORDERLY'S BUD: You're blown up, what's the fuckin' difference?

ORDERLY: The fuckin' difference is, one, you're doing a job.

ORDERLY'S BUD: And two?

ORDERLY: I dunno, man. It's stupid.

ORDERLY'S BUD: Why the hell should I go get wrecked in Iraq? I could be here having a experience. Tweakers have seen something, man. These people have got something going on, they tell you all the time. My sister? She's like, she is so fucked up! She's telling me about how I — I —

*(He collapses in a kind of laughter.)*

ORDERLY: Your sister fuckin' stole your clock radio and now you can't get up in the morning.

ORDERLY'S BUD: I don't wanna get up in the morning. To go work in the fucking mall? With no visitors even anymore? *(He takes a hit.)* How do you get up in the morning, you got the shittiest job I know of.

ORDERLY: Don't dis my job.

ORDERLY'S BUD: Your job is shit.

ORDERLY: I'm in the medical profession, man, it's a profession.

ORDERLY'S BUD: All our jobs is shit, or cleaning up shit, like yours.

*(Beat.)*

ORDERLY: I don't mind. I mean, I do, but . . . it's not just that, man.

I dunno, these old people, these old people, right? Some of 'em are fucked up, but I like 'em, y'know. I like helping 'em. I know it's just a job, man, but I dunno, they — they had lives, y'know. With jobs and insurance and houses an' shit. Like normal people, and now they're normal old. What's that anymore, man? You know anybody does that? Everybody hates their parents.

Goes out and tweaks.

Blows up their house.

All these houses, half the town, blowing up.

ORDERLY'S BUD: Blam! Pow!

*(He collapses in giggles.)*

ORDERLY: Dudes up and joining the army.

'cause your house could blow up or *you* could, OK,

*(He laughs.)*

so what's the difference

by the side of some road in some far-off craziness place

or get to the emergency room all burnt and in shreds, OK

rather clean up some old guy's pee.

Listen to his crazy stories.

Try ta get some kinda clue

how people s'pposed ta be.

*(Beat.)*

Never mind. Just don't tweak, man, 'k? 'Cause I just don't know what I'd —

ORDERLY'S BUD: Yeah, one per family, man. Plus, that'll suck if I ended up stealing my own TV.

ORDERLY: I thought you got it chained down.

ORDERLY'S BUD: Yeah, but dude. I'm the one with the key.

# THREE CHANGES
Nicky Silver

Dramatic
Hal, forties
Nate, forties

> *Hal and Nate are brothers. Nate is a success in the financial industry. Hal was a successful writer but cracked up and now is destitute. He has asked for a place to stay while he gets his life back together. The brothers have always had a contentious relationship. Hal is not only imposing upon his brother and his wife, but he has also brought in a young gay hustler to live there, too. He is, or claims to be, writing a book.*

> *(It's the middle of the night. Hal is working at the computer. The room is dark, but for some moonlight and the glow of the computer screen. After a moment, Nate enters quietly wearing pajamas, a bathrobe, and glasses. He watches Hal a moment before he speaks. They talk quietly, so as not to wake anyone. Nate seems tired, beaten.)*

NATE: I remember, when we were kids, I would watch you writing sometimes.

HAL: Nathan?

NATE: Even then, you knew what you wanted. You always did.

HAL: That's true.

NATE: Where's Gordon?

HAL: He went out.

NATE: At this time of night?

HAL: He keeps young people's hours.

NATE: Oh.

HAL: Why are you up?

NATE: I can't sleep.

HAL: Did you take a pill?

NATE: I don't like them.

HAL: You should take a pill.

NATE: They give me headaches.

HAL: The doctor said so.

NATE: I don't care.

HAL: They're perfectly safe.

NATE: I don't need to sleep.

HAL: Everyone does.

NATE: What's the difference if I sleep or not?

HAL: You'd feel better.

NATE: *(Somewhat hostile.)* No, I wouldn't.

HAL: You just want to argue.

NATE: Maybe. Probably. Are you nice to me — in the book? Do I come off as a decent person?

HAL: I don't judge my characters.

NATE: I'll take that as a no. When can I read it?

HAL: When it's finished.

NATE: When will that be?

HAL: I'm not sure. If you can't sleep, maybe you should watch TV.

NATE: I'd wake up Laurel. And besides, there's nothing good to watch.

HAL: You get two hundred channels.

NATE: I like Home Shopping. Did you ever watch Home Shopping? I don't buy anything, but I find it very soothing. Everyone is cheerful all the time. And they have jewelry with all kinds of stones, gems with names I've never heard of. I think they make up the names. Do you think that's legal?

HAL: I have no idea.

NATE: It couldn't be legal.

HAL: Do you want to play cards?

NATE: You cheat.

HAL: So do you.

NATE: *(Amused.)* I know it.

HAL: Are you hungry?

NATE: I keep thinking, I'm trying to remember where I saw it —

NATE: What?

NATE: Some movie, but I can't remember the name.

HAL: What are you talking about?

NATE: There was a scene where a photographer was surrounded by natives, African natives, or maybe they were Chinese. I can't remember. And this photographer wanted to take their picture. But the natives — or the Chinese people — wouldn't let him — or her — the photographer. They wouldn't let the photographer take their picture. They explained that they believed taking a person's picture, robbed them of their soul. Their soul left them and went into the photograph. Does that sound familiar?

HAL: No.

NATE: Maybe they were American Indian.

HAL: Who?

NATE: The people who didn't want their picture taken.

HAL: I really don't know.

NATE: It's stupid, of course. Because if we have a soul, and I'm not at all sure that we do — you think we do, don't you?

HAL: Yes.

NATE: That's right, you claim to have Jesus — or something. Anyway, if we have a soul, I don't think it just comes and goes. I mean it's ours. We own it. Don't we?

HAL: I think you have it backwards.

NATE: What?

HAL: You seem to think we own our souls. As if we're merely bodies.

NATE: I don't understand.

HAL: Should I explain it?

NATE: No. No thank you.

HAL: Then, I should get back to work.

NATE: You were always smarter than me.

HAL: You were better at some things.

NATE: Actually, no. I wasn't.

HAL: Everyone has something —

NATE: You were the star. I followed after you, like some little turd.

HAL: That's not true.

NATE: Smarter, better looking, better athlete.

HAL: I don't remember it that way. Not at all.

NATE: Remember Field Day, at school? No classes — races, athletic events on the field?

HAL: Vaguely.

NATE: You won things. People liked watching you.

HAL: Well —

NATE: I should have hated your guts. And at home, God. Do you remember we had that tetherball court?

HAL: No.

NATE: In the backyard. The tetherball court?

HAL: In the backyard?

NATE: Think.

HAL: I'm sorry, nothing.

NATE: You have to. You have to remember it.

HAL: I don't.

NATE: *(Growing agitated.)* There was the big tree, a weeping willow, and to the right, facing the house, there was a tetherball court. Concrete, a yellow ball.

HAL: All right.

NATE: Well, don't just agree.

HAL: I don't remember it.

NATE: You're lying. I don't know why — but you're lying. You remember it.

HAL: Did we use it together. Did we play together?

NATE: Not really. Not often.

HAL: Well, then.

NATE: But sometimes. When Mom sent us out, just to get out. You never wanted to play. You wanted to be off, on your own, with your friends. What was I? Your little brother. Do you remember the time, it was starting to rain, and we were playing, and you were older and better at it and you could hit it really hard. And the ball was slippery and I missed it and it hit my head, it hit my eye.

HAL: When was this?

NATE: And I went down, onto the grass.

HAL: I don't remember.

NATE: And it started to rain and my eye was bleeding. I could taste it. But I didn't cry. I wouldn't cry.

HAL: It never happened.

NATE: It did! And after that, I practiced. All the time. By myself. I wanted to beat you so bad. It's all I cared about.

HAL: Did you? Beat me?

NATE: *(Disturbed.)* . . . I don't know. I can't remember. After that, you left. You went out, into the world, and made things. You mattered.

HAL: It was a long time ago.

NATE: *(Breaking.)* All I wanted — was for you to like me.

HAL: I did.

NATE: You were my brother.

HAL: *(Gentle.)* I did like you.

NATE: You cut us dead.

HAL: You should lie down.

NATE: I needed you to love me.

HAL: *(Gentle.)* I do.

NATE: That's all.

HAL: I do love you, Nate. Of course I do.
    *(Beat.)*

NATE: One day, when you were out, I looked at what you're writing.

HAL: Oh?

NATE: I didn't read much. Just a page. But it was good. Really . . . It was beautiful.

HAL: *(Warm.)* Thank you.

*(Beat.)*

NATE: What happened to your glasses?

HAL: I lost them.

NATE: You don't need them?

HAL: It seems I don't.

NATE: You can see?

HAL: Perfectly. Isn't that amazing? I've worn glasses for years.

NATE: *(Disturbed.)* . . . I'm going to lie down now.

HAL: Good.

*(Nate exits. Hal returns to work.)*

# WHAT TO DO WHEN YOU HATE ALL YOUR FRIENDS
Larry Kunofsky

Comic
Matt, maybe late twenties, maybe early thirties
Garrett, same age

> *Matt and Garrett have known each other for years. Here, as the play be-*
> *gins, they are sitting in their familiar haunt, a cafe/restaurant. Matt has*
> *just come to the conclusion that he has no friends. Garrett refuses to ac-*
> *cept this. If your friend has no friends, well . . . who are you, then?*

*(Matt and Garrett are seated together by a restaurant table.)*
MATT: I have no friends.
GARRETT: What are you saying.
MATT: I'm saying: "I have no friends."
GARRETT: You mean you don't have as many friends as you used to have.
MATT: That's true. Because now I have *no* friends.
GARRETT: You have plenty of friends.
MATT: By plenty, do you mean none?
GARRETT: You have a myriad of friends.
MATT: I have no friends.
GARRETT: You have a plethora of friends.
MATT: I have no friends.
GARRETT: What are you saying.
MATT: What part of "I Have No Friends" remains unclear to you.
GARRETT: *(Thinks.)* Wow.
MATT: I know.
GARRETT: What about Frank?
MATT: Frank is not my friend.
GARRETT: *(Thinks.)* That's true. Frank is not your friend. What about Dave?
MATT: Dave Berlin or Dave Romany?
GARRETT: Dave Romany.
MATT: Dave Romany is a tool.
GARRETT: Yeah. What about Dave Berlin?
MATT: Tool.

GARRETT: Yeah. Arnold. Bo. Assaf. Porter. Shorty.

MATT: No. No. No. No. And no.

GARRETT: Tim.

MATT: Tim's dead.

GARRETT: Oh my God. I didn't know Tim was dead. Tim was a good friend.

MATT: Tim wasn't a friend at all. I have no friends.

GARRETT: Well he was a good friend to me.

MATT: You didn't even know he was dead.

GARRETT: We weren't close.

MATT: You weren't friends.

GARRETT: Hey. Tim and me. Although not close. Were tight.

MATT: Would you have gone to the funeral?

GARRETT: What about Ignacio.

MATT: Ignacio was *your* friend.

GARRETT: He still *is* my friend.

MATT: You *have* no friends.

GARRETT: Now *I* have no friends?

MATT: Think about it.

# YEAR ZERO
## Michael Golamco

Dramatic
Vuthy (pronounced "woo-tee"), sixteen
Han, late twenties

> *Vuthy, a Cambodian American, is a small, skinny kid struggling to grow
> up in a rough part of Los Angeles. He has been getting beat up every day
> at school. Han's solution is to "man him up" by taking him to a local
> house of prostitution. Han, also Cambodian American, is a high-rank-
> ing gang member and Vuthy's unofficial elder brother and protector.*

> *(A suburban brothel. A doorway with a beaded curtain, colored lights.
> A chair sits nearby. Sound of a baseball game on TV. Han walks through the
> beaded curtain. Vuthy pauses behind it.)*

HAN: Get in here.

> *(Han puts an arm through the curtain, pulls Vuthy through.)*

VUTHY: *(Looking around.)* Oh. Jeez.

HAN: Yeah.

VUTHY: Manny Nguyen at school always said this house was a ho house. I
didn't believe him.

HAN: Well Manny Nguyen was right.

VUTHY: Thass funny — it looks just like a regular house on the outside —

HAN: Yeah, I don't know how they do it. Must be magic. *(Points straight
ahead.)* Choose one.

VUTHY: What? . . . No, man — I can't —

HAN: I got you. Don't worry about it —

VUTHY: No —

HAN: Just choose one of these girls. I got you.

> *(Vuthy presses his face into Han's shoulder, embarrassed.)*

VUTHY: I can't, man.

HAN: Why not?

VUTHY: I'm shy.

HAN: Fuck you, you're shy. Choose one of these girls before I hit you.

> *(Vuthy laughs awkwardly.)*

VUTHY: I've never done it before —

HAN: Thass kinda the point.

VUTHY: Han —

HAN: Choose one or I'll chose one for you.

VUTHY: This is weird.

HAN: What's weird about it? They're selling, you're buying. Look. If you don't like any of the ones here, I know another place. Though it's a lot more fobby —

VUTHY: OK — OK.

*(He nervously scans around. Han points.)*

HAN: How 'bout her.

VUTHY: She's a little too old.

HAN: Her.

VUTHY: She looks like an alien.

HAN: OK, her.

VUTHY: She looks too much like Ra. Oh shit — was that fucked up of me to say?

HAN: No, I feel you. How 'bout her — she's a stunner —

VUTHY: No — she's too cute. I'd nut too quick —

HAN: Thass OK. First time around, every dude lasts like five seconds. So I got you covered for two rounds. The first time, don't worry about shootin' one off. Then you can relax, hit it a second time, and get into it once the pressure's off —

VUTHY: What are you gonna do?

HAN: Don't worry about me. The Dodger game's on.

*(Vuthy spots someone at the far end of the room.)*

VUTHY: Oh shit.

HAN: What?

VUTHY: Thass Heidi Trang!

HAN: Who?

VUTHY: Heidi Trang. She was like, a senior when I was a freshman.

HAN: Oh. Yeah, Heidi.

VUTHY: Shit — she's a ho now?

HAN: Everybody got their own destination. So you wanna put your *kahldol* *(Pronounced kah-DAH.)* in her or what?

VUTHY: Shit, Han — I can't.

HAN: Why not?

VUTHY: She was runner-up for prom queen —

HAN: So what?

VUTHY: Han —

HAN: Thass it — she's the one. You're doing her on principle. *(Beat)* Don't worry, she's good.

VUTHY: You? —

HAN: Yeah. *(He puts up a hand, motions over.)* Yeah, Heidi! This young buck here wants to meet you. *(He takes a couple of condoms out of his pocket, hands them to Vuthy.)* Go.

*(Vuthy steps forward slowly, freezes.)*

VUTHY: Han —

HAN: What now?

VUTHY: I never even . . . I never —

HAN: What?

VUTHY: I never even kissed a girl before.

HAN: Oh. Well, that's the one thing you can't do here: You can't kiss 'em. *(Grinning.)* And that's probably the only thing you can't do here —

VUTHY: No.

HAN: No what?

VUTHY: No, that's . . . I wanna save that for . . . I want that to be special.

*(Han studies him, puzzled, then gets it.)*

HAN: OK. No kissing then. *(Beat.)* So go. I'll be right here.

*(Vuthy self-consciously steps forward into the darkness. Han sits in the chair, lights a cigarette. He takes a few puffs, checks out the baseball game on TV. To someone nearby:)*

HAN: So. What's the score?

# RIGHTS AND PERMISSIONS

The complete text of every play in this volume is available from the performance rights holder, except as otherwise noted.

*Note:* **For playwrights whose names are followed by an asterisk (\*), information can be found about them on the "Meet Our Authors" web page at www.smithandkraus.com.**

### MONOLOGUES

ACCORDING TO GOLDMAN © 2008 by Bruce Graham. Reprinted by permission of Mary Harden, Harden-Curtis Assoc.. For performance rights, contact Dramatists Play Service, 440 Park Ave. S., New York, NY 10016 (www.dramatists.com) (212-683-8960).

ALOHA SAY THE PRETTY GIRLS © 2008 by Naomi Iizuka. Reprinted by permission of Morgan Jenness, Abrams Artists Agency. For performance rights, contact Playscripts, Inc., 450 7th Ave. #803, New York, NY 10123. (www.playscripts.com) (866-639-7529).

AMERICAN TET © 2008 by Lydia Stryk.* Reprinted by permission of the author. For performance rights, contact Broadway Play Publishing, 56 E. 81st St., New York, NY 10021 (www.broadwayplaypubl.com) (212-772-8334).

AND THE WINNER IS © 2008 by Mitch Albom.* Reprinted by permission of David Black, David Black Agency. For performance rights, contact Dramatists Play Service, 440 Park Ave. S., New York, NY 10016 (www.dramatists.com) (212-683-8960).

BACK BACK BACK © 2008 by Itamar Moses.* Reprinted by permission of Farrar, Straus & Giroux LLC. For performance rights, contact Samuel French, Inc. (www.samuelfrench.com) (212-206-8990).

BAGGAGE © by Sam Bobrick.* Reprinted by permission of the author. For performance rights, contact Samuel French, Inc. (www.samuel french .com) (212-206-8990).

BILLBOARD © 2008 by Michael Vukadinovich.* Reprinted by permission of the author. For performance rights, contact Samuel French, Inc. (www.samuelfrench.com) (212-206-8990).

DUCK HUNTER SHOOTS ANGEL © 2008 by Mitch Albom.* Reprinted by permission of David Black, David Black Agency. For performance rights, contact Dramatists Play Service, 440 Park Ave. S., New York, NY 10016 (www.dramatists.com) (212-683-8960).

EQUIVOCATION © 2008 by Bill Cane. Reprinted by permission of Beth Blickers, Abrams Artists Agency. For performance rights, contact Beth Blickers (beth.blickers@abramsartny.com).

ESSENTIAL SELF-DEFENSE © 2008 by Adam Rapp. Reprinted by permission of Farrar, Straus & Giroux LLC. For performance rights, contact Broadway Play Publishing, 56 E. 81st St., New York, NY 10021 (www.broadwayplaypubl.com) (212-772-8334).

FAULT LINES © 2008 by Stephen Belber. Reprinted by permission of John Buzzetti, The Gersh Agency. For performance rights, contact Dramatists Play Service, 440 Park Ave. S., New York, NY 10016 (www.dramatists .com (212-683-8960).

50 WORDS © 2008 by Michael Weller. Reprinted by permission of Tiffany Mischeshin, Theatre Communications Group. For performance rights, contact Dramatists Play Service, 440 Park Ave. S., New York, NY 10016 (www.dramatists.com) (212-683-8960).

FROM UP HERE © 2008 by Liz Flahive.* Reprinted by permission of Val Day, William Morris Endeavor Entertainment. For performance rights, contact Samuel French, Inc. (www.samuelfrench.com) (212-206-8990).

GOOD BOYS AND TRUE © 2008 by Roberto Aguirre-Sacasa. Reprinted by permission of John Buzzetti, The Gersh Agency. For performance rights, contact Dramatists Play Service, 440 Park Ave. S., New York, NY 10016 (www.dramatists.com) (212-683-8960).

SCENES